I0455876

Northern Boy

Northern Boy

Alan Feltus

Copyright © 2009 by Alan Feltus.

ISBN: Softcover   978-1-4500-1174-7
               ebook   978-1-4500-0267-7

All rights reserved. No part of this book may be reproduced or
transmitted in any form or by any means, electronic or mechanical,
including photocopying, recording, or by any information storage
and retrieval system, without permission in writing from the
copyright owner.

This book was printed in the United States of America.

To order additional copies of this book, contact:
Xlibris Corporation
1-888-795-4274
www.Xlibris.com
Orders@Xlibris.com
72633

CHAPTER 1

We moved from a small town in northern Minnesota to a small country house sitting in the middle of a 120 acre field. The closest town was eight miles away, so needless to say, I spent a lot of time by myself. Both of my parents worked and I had no way of going anywhere. It wasn't that bad. There was a small creek that ran through the field and I spent a lot of time there catching frogs and tadpoles and just doing kid stuff. This creek was maybe two feet across and about a foot deep, so my parents never really worried too much about me being there by myself. I learned a lot about nature sitting down there. I'd watch the different kinds of birds that built their nests in the bull rushes and in the few trees that grew along the edge of the creek . . . listening to their songs and seeing them feed their young. I would wade in the water picking up stones that might look interesting and looking to see what kind of bugs that lived under them.

One day, I was sitting on the bank of this creek and saw this really ugly bug crawling up on a cattail that was growing next to me. I had never seen anything like it before. I wondered what it was and would it bite me if I tried to pick it up? So, I decided to just watch and see what it was doing. It took awhile, but what I saw was just amazing! This bug crawled up maybe a few inches out of the water and just sat there for awhile. Then the outside of the bug started to split open. To my amazement, a pair of wings popped out followed by a long skinny body. What I was watching was the birth of a dragonfly. A lot of people would say big deal, so what, and that they're not interested in this. But I tell you what! It was one of the coolest things I had ever seen. After it was completely out of its old shell it again just sat there drying itself in the warm summer air . . . stretching its wings moving them up and down. A little while later it started beating it wings and flew off. It was over just as fast as it started, but left me with a memory of its birth.

In this short stretch of creek that I was able to go to, was a small pool of water. Depending on what time of day I was there, I would see bugs land on the water. Just as fast as they would land, something would come up from below and snatch it off the top of the water. I knew there were small minnows in this creek, I'd seen many of them. My step-father told me they were Chub minnows. But some of those bugs were larger than the little fish I had seen. Like large adult grasshoppers, they were a couple of inches long with long legs and wings. Butterflies or bumble bees, if they landed in this pool, whatever it was that was in there, was eating them. I was telling my step-father about this and he really did not seem too interested in what I had to say, but he gave me this old fishing rod that had no reel on it and missing a couple of eyes. He had tied about six feet of fishing line on the top eye and then tied a small fishing hook on the other end of the line. He told me to go down to the small garden we had and dig up some of the weeds that grew there, and as long as I was there, to pick up the small earthworms that I would find. So I got an old empty soup can, put some dirt in it, and went and dug up the weeds. I found a lot of these small pink earthworms and put them in the can. The next day I took my pole and worms down to that pool. It was early in the morning, there was dew still on the grass and an early morning fog over the water. I found a small flat rock to sit on and watched the water to see if there was anything swimming in the pool. I took one of the small pink worms I had dug up and tossed it in the water. It no sooner hit the water and there was a large swirl and the worm disappeared. So I put another one of those pink worms on the hook that was tied onto my fishing line and tossed it into the water. Just like before, as soon as the worm hit the water, there was this swirl of water and the worm was gone. All of a sudden my fishing pole was jerking around all over the place and there was this fish splashing, jumping out of the water, just going crazy trying to get rid of the hook that was stuck in its mouth. This was so exciting, my heart was beating like crazy! I strode up with my fishing pole in my hand and was trying to get this fish out of the water. Because the line was tied on to the top eye of the pole, I was having a hard time lifting it out of the water. In all my excitement I had slipped and both feet ended up in the water, which ended up to be for the best. I tossed my pole in the grass, hanging on to the fishing line, I was able to lead the fish into the grass by the edge of the pool, slid my hand under it and picked it up. I had no idea what a Chub looked like, I just knew they were in this water because my step-father said they were. Were they good to eat or do I just let them go? All I knew was, this fish was much larger than most of the other fish I had seen in this creek. This fish was at least a foot long. When I held it up and looked at it, it had the most wonderful colors I had ever seen on a fish. There were red spots with blue around them, there were blue spots with red around them and the fins were red with a white stripe down the edge. The back was a dark green with what looked like worm tracks running through it, and they were all just so sharp and bright.

So, I thought I would take it home and show my mother. I picked up my stuff and headed back to the house. When I got back, I put my worms and fishing pole in the shed out back of the house. Then I headed in to show my mom what I had caught. My step-father was in his usual place in the kitchen, sitting, having a beer, and watching football. That's where he spent a lot of time during the weekends. The kitchen sink was clear, so I put my fish in it, ran a little water on it, and went and got my mom to take a look at this fish I had caught. She humored me and came in the kitchen and looked at the fish. She picked it up with a surprised look on her face, turned around and held it up so that my step-father could see it. At first, he just kind of looked past it, watching his game, and then, I don't know, maybe he focused in on what my mom was trying to show him. He sat back in his chair, took a drink of his beer, then took the fish from my mom's hand, and turned to looked at me. At first I thought I had done something wrong. He had this strange look on his face. Then after a few seconds that seemed like minutes, he says, "where did you catch this fish"? I looked at him and told him "down at the small pool in the creek". Then I asked him if I had done something wrong? He just looked at me and kind of chuckled to himself and told me that the fish that I caught was called a Brook Trout, and they were very good eating. He said that if he had known they were in that creek he would have been down there fishing himself. He got out of his chair, grabbed a small paring knife, and told me to follow him outside. Once we got out there, he knelt in the grass and said if I was going to go catch these fish that I should know how to clean them so they didn't go to waste. He took the knife and opened it up so he could get all the insides out. He did it so fast that I hardly saw how he did it. Then back in the house to the sink. He washed the fish out so that there was no blood or anything else left inside. The inside of this fish was a beautiful orangish red, and he told me that was the way they were supposed look. Then he took out a freezer bag put the fish in it and threw it in the freezer. Then he says that as soon as I caught enough for everyone, that we would have them for supper. After that he went and sat back down, took another drink of his beer, and started watching the game on TV. My mom went back to doing what she was doing and I went back outside. It was still early, so I thought I would go back to the creek. I grabbed my pole and the can of worms and headed back through the field towards the pool. I was just about there when I saw a large deer standing in the pool. I stopped in my tracks and watched what it was doing. It was drinking water and every once in awhile it would pick up its head and look around. I could see its large ears moving around, listening for different sounds. It kept looking in the brush that was growing on the other side. As I watched, all of a sudden there was another deer walking out of that brush. Then to my surprise, a third deer stood up. It had been lying down in the tall grass and even though I had been looking right at them, I had not seen it until it stood up. It was then I understood that I was not the only one using that pool. Well, I don't know what I did, if anything, but all three of those deer stopped what they were doing and started looking right at me. The deer that was in the pool turned, put its tail in the air, and all three of them disappeared into the brush. I walked the rest of the way there, looking and listening, to see if they were still around. But I didn't see or hear anything but the birds that lived there.

I got back by the edge of the pool and sat down on the same rock I had found earlier that morning. I put another pink worm on the hook and tossed it in the water, wondering if another fish was going to eat it like before. But nothing happened.

Now the sun was high in the sky and the water was clear enough that I could see my worm lying on the bottom of the pool. After watching for a little bit, I saw that there were no fish in there either. Well, I really did not feel like going home just then, so I left my line in the water and started looking for something better to sit on.

There were several larger trees that had died and had fallen down over time. They were covered with green moss and broke into smaller pieces when I tried to pick them up. I took several of the smaller pieces and moved them over by the pool were I was fishing. In the process, when I picked up the logs, I saw that the dirt under them had small pink worms in it. This was a good thing! Now I knew that if I needed worms to fish with, I no longer needed to go dig up weeds in the garden. I could just kick over dead old logs and find them. A lot easier to do.

After making myself a better place to sit, I started looking around the pool to see what those deer were doing down there. There was a small spot with no grass, just mud, and in that mud I found a few tracks. It had been right where the deer were standing. These were the first deer tracks I had ever seen. Then I noticed that there was what looked like a trail that went right along the edge of the creek. So me being me, I followed it to see where it went. It followed the creek right up to the edge of the woods at the end of the field. That's where I had to stop. I was told not to go into the woods for any reason. The creek kept going into the woods and so did the path I was on, but I turned around and headed back to the pool. It was getting late and I was getting hungry by then, so I grabbed my stuff and headed back to the house.

On my way, I turned around and was looking across the field to the edge of the woods by where I had been, and I could see several deer feeding in the field. I never knew that there were so many animals that lived by us.

That night after it was dark, I was sitting in my room reading a book, when my step father called for me. I went into the kitchen and he told me to have a seat. On the table were a flashlight and a Styrofoam bucket. He was standing at the sink with his back to me, and when he turned around, his hands were full of wet shredded paper that he put into the bucket. I asked him what he was doing and he simply told me that he was making up a bait box. I must have looked a little bit puzzled. He told me that shredded paper was better than dirt to put worms in, that they fed on the print and it was easier for them to move around in. Then he told me to take the flashlight and follow him down to the garden. Well, ok. I had no idea what was going on but I soon found out. When we got by the garden he traded me the bucket for the light. He told me to stay on the grass and he started shining the light down on the ground in front of him. I then found out what he was doing. In the light I could see these huge worms on the top of the dirt. But these were not just any worms, these worms were fast! When he would go to grab one, it would disappear back into its hole faster than you could blink an eye. But with timing, he soon had several in the bucket. He told me that if you grab one and it breaks, to just let it go and find another. That if you put a broken worm in the bucket it would soon die and then the rest of them would die also. So, he handed me the bucket and told me to have fun, turned, walked away, and went back in the house. It took awhile, but I figured out how to grab them before they had a chance to get away. By shining the light so it did not shine directly on them I was able to grab a hold of them. By pulling easy until they came out of their hole, I soon was not breaking very many of them. I went through the garden and had caught maybe a couple dozen. I headed back to the house. On the way, I shined the light out in the field and there were eyes shining back at me all over the place! The field was now full of deer feeding on the grass and clover that grew out there. They did not seem to care that I was watching them. I went into the house, handed my step-dad the bucket and flashlight, and told him of all the deer I had just seen. He just said that they were there every night and it was time to go to bed. So I did, but I could not fall asleep. Instead, my thoughts were all about the things I had learned that day. The fish in the pool and what they were, the deer that I had seen and the trail they had followed, and then the making of a bait box and catching those huge worms. I had changed that day. I did not really know it, but I had. Not only had I changed, but so had my step father. He had talked to me, not at me, and for no real reason he showed a real interest in what I was doing. Something he had never done before. It was a long day and I fell asleep.

When I woke up it was still dark. I looked at the clock on the wall . . . 4am. Then I remembered it was Monday, my folks were getting ready to leave for work. My mom asked me what I was going to do today and I told her that after I cut the grass and put the dishes away, I thought I'd go down to the creek. She looked at me and said, "remember, from the road to the edge of the woods, no farther", and to "be careful". Then she got in her car and headed off to work. I watched the tail lights going down the driveway, turn on the main road, and then she was gone. I was all by myself for the rest of the day. Nothing new, it was that way every day.

The sky was just starting to lighten up. I loved the smell of mornings. Everything was so fresh and clean. I walked around back and checked out the field, hoping that the deer were still there, but there were none. So I went about my business . . . made something to eat, washed the few dishes that I had just dirtied, and put them all away. Then I went out and pulled the mower out of the shed. The grass had to be cut, it was getting long, and I was told to do it. Cutting the grass took half a day. We had a very large front yard and almost as much in the back. It was about an acre and a half total and all we had was a push mower, not the gas powered kind. It was hard work, but it had to be done, otherwise I got in a world of crap when my step-father got home and Lord knows that was not anything I wanted to happen.

As I was cutting the grass, I kept pushing up grasshoppers. They were thick! Then I remembered the ones I had seen jump into that pool at the creek and how they floated there. Then how that Brookie had come up and ate them. I finished cutting the grass and went out to the garage to find something to put a couple of grasshoppers in. There was a couple of baby food jars with the lids still on them, so I took one, went out back, caught four or five of them, and put them in the jar with a little grass. Then I went and grabbed my fishing pole and my can of pink worms, walked out back, and headed to the pool.

It was afternoon by that time and very sunny out. As I got closer to the pool I started watching and listening to make sure I didn't spook up any animals that might be there. Again the water was very clear and there was nothing in the pool. So now what was I going to do? I sat down on the logs that I had laid down the day before and was just kind of day dreaming. Then I thought about the two culverts that were in the creek. One had been put in where the neighbor's cows crossed the creek and the other was where the road went over the creek. I decided that the one by the road was the biggest of the two. I really did not feel like crossing a barbed wire fence and having a bunch of crazy cows chase me around. Maybe they would or maybe they wouldn't, but why take the chance? So I headed to the road and walked down to the creek. When I got there, I walked over to where the front of the culvert was and saw that the water that flowed through it was maybe two feet deep. Then I noticed just how much room I had. Not much. There were tall weeds and cattails growing almost right next to the caulvert. How was I going to get my line inside that culvert? I started looking around for a small stick or piece of wood that I could use to float my line inside. Nothing nowhere.

Then, like someone turned on a light bulb, I remembered that one day when I had been messing around at the creek, I had seen these weeds that had like little balls growing on them. I had picked a couple and threw them in the water and they floated down stream. I looked around and there were a couple of them growing nearby, but they were on the other side of that barbed wire fence. Well, I was not going to be in there very long. I just wanted a couple of those weeds and get back out. So I walked over to the fence and looked to see if there were any cows nearby. There wasn't, so I reached down, grabbed the top wire to lift it just a little, then grabbed the middle wire, and my life flashed before my eyes! My whole life lit up as a shock went through my whole body. Damn that hurt! I found out just how they kept those crazy cows in that field . . . electric fence! After I got my thoughts back together, I started looking at the fence that just woke me up, and I noticed that the center wire had these little white things on them that looked like they were made of glass. Nothing on the top or bottom wire. I held my breath and slapped the top wire. Nothing. I grabbed it and held it for a second, still nothing. Okay, so as long as I stayed away from that center wire, things would be okay. I crawled under the bottom wire and went and got what I was after. That was a heck of a price to pay for those weeds that I was not even sure would work.

Next, I still had to figure out a way to connect that round ball on my line. I took one of those round weeds and used the top of my can to cut a slice half way through it. Then I slid my line in the cut and put in part of the stem to wedge it in tight. I put it about a foot above my hook, put a worm on, tossed it in the water, and it worked! The water wasn't moving fast, but a little at a time it was drifting into that culvert and out of sight. It didn't go all that far in when I heard a splash and my fishing rod was bouncing. I pulled back and I knew that I had a fish on my line. I threw my rod down, grabbed the line, and pulled that fish in and out of the water by hand. I got it into the grass, grabbed it, and took the hook out of its lip. I looked at it and saw that it was not quite as long as the first one I had caught the day before, but it was close. And again, the colors were so neat, so bright. Brookies have such beautiful markings. I put my fish in the grass farther away from the water so it could not flop back in, rebaited my hook, and tried again. Just like the first time, it no sooner got out of sight and I heard another splash. This time I was waiting and when I heard it, I pulled my rod back. But this time there was nothing on the other end, not even my worm! A free lunch for the fish I was thinking. I went and put another worm on. It was my last pink worm. I dropped it into the water and watched it slowly drift out of sight. This time there was no splash. My line just went tight and the tip of my pole was going nuts. I pulled my rod back, just not as hard, then put my rod down and repeated what I had done before. I grabbed the line and pulled the fish in and out of the water by hand and into the grass. It was almost a twin to the other one, just a lot fatter. Now I had two very nice fish and no worms. Then I remembered the grass hoppers I had brought with me. I took the lid off from the jar [wrong]. As soon as I lifted the lid, those grasshoppers jumped out of the jar. All but one made good their escape. It took a little doing, but I ran it down and caught it again. Now, how do you hook a grasshopper? When I was looking it over, I noticed that on its back there was like a small shield where its legs all hooked together. I put my hook just under and around that shield and dropped it into the water. But it did not sink like the worms, it floated all by itself. I pulled my line out of the water and took off the round weed I was using to float my line into the culvert. I put it back in and watched it float out of sight.

I set my rod down in the grass and started looking at the two fish I had caught. I just could not help it, they just are so cool looking with all their colors. My line never moved, pole never twitched, nothing for about a half hour. My fish looked like they were drying out, so I decided to head home. Tomorrow was another day and I would get more pink worms when I got home. So I picked up my fishing pole and tried to pull my line out of the culvert, but my line was not moving. It seemed to be stuck on something inside the culvert. I put a little more pressure on my pole and there was a thump, thump. Something was pulling back hard, real hard! My pole all of a sudden started bending and my heart was just about to beat out of my chest. What the heck had I hooked in to! Then there was an explosion inside that culvert. Water was splashing, my pole was bending, my heart was beating a hundred times a second. It took me what seemed like forever to get my hands on the line. Even when I did, whatever was on my line was pulling hard and splashing around like crazy. Finally I was able to pull my line in enough to see that, yes, there was this huge fish on my hook. Then I got scared. Not afraid to touch it, but I was afraid it would get off my hook and no one would ever believe me if I told them about this fish. The first time I went to lift it out of the water it was flopping all over the place and right back into the water it went. Lucky for me, I still had a hold of the line with my other hand. The second time I lifted the fish out it was still going crazy, but I managed to get it over by where the other two fish were. And snap! The line broke! I had the fish though. I had gotten on my knees and had both hands on it. That fish was going nowhere but home.

This fish did not look like the other ones I had in the grass. Well it did, but it didn't. It had these big colored spots on it, but it was a different color and it looked like scales on it, where the Brookies were smooth. And teeth! Lots of sharp little teeth. Not to mention that this fish was like three or four times as big. It was without a doubt the very biggest fish I had ever caught. Not that I had caught a lot of fish, but I was excited. I slid my fingers into the gills of these fish, grabbed my stuff, and home I went.

As I was walking up the road heading for the drive way, a car went by, slowed down, turned around, and came back by. The car stopped and this guy got out and started walking towards me. This made me very nervous. I had no idea who he was or what he wanted. He got closer and I could see a smile on his face which made me feel a little bit easier. Then he said "nice fish you have there kid". I said "thank you" and he asked me where I had caught them. I pointed down at the creek. I saw him looking at my fishing pole and kind of smiling. He asked me where I lived and by that time you could see the house from where we were. I pointed again up at the house this time. He told me his name and something else that I did not understand, then he explained that it was his job to measure and weigh fish that people caught and that he was heading some place else when he saw me walking with these fish. He asked me if he could check out my fish and I nodded my head and said sure. We went up to his car, he opened the trunk, and pulled out this book. He started writing down a bunch of stuff, then he took out this long measuring stick and asked me to lay the biggest fish next to it. I did and he wrote down some more stuff in his book. He asked me if I knew what kind of fish I had caught. I told him I knew the two smaller ones were Brook Trout but I had no idea what the bigger one was. He dug around in a box of stuff he had in his trunk and he found a small book that had a bunch of pictures of different fish. He turned to a page and showed me a picture of the same kind of fish. He goes "that big fish you caught is called a German Brown Trout". He told me that he had no idea that there were Browns that large in these small creeks. Then he asked me about my fishing pole and I explained to him that this was my first pole and that my step-father had given it to me. He just looked at me and smiled then said "thank you for your time", got in his car, turned around, and left.

I went back to the house, put my stuff away, and went and got the same paring knife my step-dad used. I opened up the fish like he did, took everything out of them, and washed them out. I got the freezer bag out of the freezer and put the two Brook Trout in it, sealed it up, and put it back in the freezer. I had no idea what to do with this German Brown, it was way too big. I opened a drawer and inside there were some empty bread bags. I put my fish in one, but it was not big enough to close, so I put a second bag on the fish from the other direction and then put it in the freezer. Then I went and washed up my hands. They were full of fish slime and smelled really bad, just like fish . . . image that!

I went outside and got my can from the shed and went down to the garden. I grabbed the shovel and started digging weeds and sifting through the dirt looking for more worms. I had just finished and was heading to the shed to put my can back so they would stay cool, when I heard the truck coming up the drive way. It was my step-father coming home from work. I wanted to tell him what had happened today but I knew to wait for awhile until he had a chance to wind down and have a beer or two. So I just kept doing what I had been doing. I had just shut the door on the shed when I heard the porch door open and he called me over. I went over to ask him what he wanted and he asked me if I had gone down to the creek today. I nodded my head and answered yes, I had. He then asked me if I had caught any fish. Again, I nodded my head and said yes. He asked me what I had done with them. I told him that I had cleaned them the same way that he had showed me and that I had put two of the fish in the freezer bag, but I did not know what to do with the larger one. He did not say anything, he just turned around and went straight to the freezer, opened it, and looked inside. I heard the freezer door shut and him call my name. I had heard that tone of voice before and it was never a good thing. I knew something was up. I had no choice but to walk into the kitchen. I looked at him and said "yes"? He said "where were you today"? I could see that big Brown Trout laying in the sink. "Down to the creek", I replied, and he flat out called me a liar. He says "there is no way in hell that you caught that fish in that creek". So again, he asked me where had I been today, and again I had told him that I had gone down to the creek. He slammed his hand down on the table hard and said to get out of his face. "Damn liar"! He goes, "don't go anywhere, your mother is going to want to talk to you". I went and sat outside and stayed out of sight. A little while later I heard my mom's car coming up the driveway. I stayed out of sight because I knew what was going to happen next and I was not wrong. I heard them screaming at each other, and again, this was nothing new. They fought with each other a lot. But this time, I heard my name mentioned and I knew that it was all about me. I did not know what I had done that was so wrong. I had done my chores, stayed were I was supposed to, and even cleaned up the mess I had made with the fish I had caught. Then I heard him say that he did not want me leaving the yard until I told them where I had gone today. And again, I heard him call me a damn liar. That hurt, because all I ever did was try to make that man like me, but nothing I ever did was good enough for him. I had thought that things were going to be different. He had actually talked to me and showed some interest in what I was doing, but that was short lived.

A little while later after things had quieted down, I heard the porch door shut. I thought, ok, what next? I wasn't moving from where I was. Then I heard footsteps coming up behind me and I turned to see my mother standing there. She looked at me and I could see that she had been crying. That hurt me. Even more, I hated when he made her cry. She sat down next to me and looked me right in the eyes and asked me "where did you catch that fish"? I looked at her and said "down at the creek". "Honest mom, I did not go any place I was not supposed to go". I could feel a tear rolling down my cheek. "I thought that he would be happy for me". I told her "if I had known that this was going to happen, I would have let that stupid fish go". She just sat there not saying anything, then she put her hand on my arm, gave it a little squeeze, and said that she believed me. I turned and gave her a big hug and said "thank you". Then she told me that I was grounded to the yard for awhile. I understood that it was not something she wanted to do, but to keep peace in the house it was something that had to happen. She got up and walked quietly into the house. There were a few words exchanged between them and then it was quiet. I stayed outside until dark before I went in, then I just went to bed. The rest of the week I kept a very low profile until they both had left for work. I did my chores and stayed in the yard like I was told to do.

It was a very long week and all I could think about was that creek and the fish that were in it. I don't know why, but I wanted to go back there really bad, it was like I was obsessed with the thought. Saturday came and I thought to myself "great, I had to stay in the yard and my step-dad was going to be home all day". I wondered what he was going to find today that I had done wrong. I was not going to give him the chance to get mad at me. I had noticed that the grass had to be cut, so instead of waiting to be told to cut it, I would just do it. I went and pulled the mower out of the shed and started cutting the grass. I had about half of the front yard cut when I saw this car driving up the driveway. It looked familiar, but then again, I was not sure. I just figured it was someone who knew my folks. The man driving waved as he went by. I waved back and just kept cutting the grass. When I finished, I cleaned the mower off and put it back in the shed. I noticed that whoever had driven up to the house was gone. Then I heard my mother call my name, so I went into the house to see what she wanted. When I walked into the kitchen both my mom and my step-dad were sitting at the table. I just stood there not saying anything but rather waiting to find out what they wanted. Mom was looking at my step-dad, not saying anything, but you could see that she was waiting for him to say something. Then he turned in his chair and ask me if I had seen the car drive up to the house? "Yes", I said. Then he asked me if I knew who he was? I said "no, not really". He then asked me if I remembered a car stopping on the road when I was coming back from the creek? Then it dawned on me where I had seen that man before. I said "yes" and that "he wanted to see how big my fish were" and that "he had told me that it was his job". "Then he had showed me a picture of the fish I had just caught, he called it a German Brown". He asked me why I had not said anything before this about seeing that guy. I looked at the floor and answered softly, "you never gave me a chance to say anything" "You told me to get out of your face and said that I was lying to you". Well, he said, "that guy was called a fish enumerator" and "yes, it was his job to see what kind of fish and what size of fish people were catching". If it was not for the fact that he had come up to the house and explained that he had indeed seen me on the road and had stopped me to check out my fish and that the fish was still alive when he measured it, he still wouldn't have believed me. Neither the man or my step-dad would have believed that a trout that size could have been in that little creek. This was my step-father's way of saying he was sorry for calling me a liar without coming straight out and saying that he had made a mistake. I understood this because he never made mistakes. According to him. "Anyway", he continued, "the guy had noticed your fishing rod and had come up to the house to ask if we minded if he gave you a different one" and that "he also belonged to a group of people who worked with kids. He took them fishing, and camping, things like that". Both my folks agreed that it was ok and the man had dropped off a box of stuff just for me. It was in the living room. Inside that box there were a lot of things, but right on top was the same book that he had showed me that had the picture of my fish in it. On the outside of the book it said *Guide to Stream Trout Lakes in Minnesota*. Under that was this red tackle box. When I opened it there were hooks of different sizes, a round spool of line, a fish stringer to put fish on, and a handful of small round sinkers. On the outside of the box was a ruler that was made right into the box. On the very bottom of the box was a small metal box with a lid on it and two loops so you could wear it on your belt. It was green and said Bait Box on the top. When I had looked at all the stuff in the box, I turned to show it to my parents. Leaning against the wall right by the door was a brand new fishing rod and reel, still in the wrapper! I did not know what to say. I was so happy that I almost started to cry. I had never had anyone give me anything like this before. My step-father told me to go back outside and that later he would show me how to set things up. I grabbed my new book and went back outside. I went over by this big oak tree that was in the yard, sat down, opened it up, and started looking at all the different pictures of fish that were in it. This was just the beginning. I was hooked for life. I knew I would never starve. How does that saying go? Give a man a fish and he will have a meal, teach him to fish and he will never go hungry . . .

Chapter 2

It seems like a lifetime since we moved out here and I started fishing that little creek, but it's only been a few years. I now know almost every inch of that feeder creek. From the spring where it starts to the Midway River that it empties in to. I just had my 12th birthday and my step-father gave me a single shot .28 gauge shot gun. Small game season will be opening up soon and I have been reading everything I can lay my hands on about gray squirrels, partridge, and rabbits. I have walked the trails watching, listening, and learning as much as possible. Early in the mornings and at dusk I learned that if you walk the edge of the field you can catch the partridge sitting in the trees. In the afternoons you can walk the trails and see them eating small rocks and gravel to help them grind up their food that they have in their crop, or hanging out by the small pot holes that hold water. They eat a lot of things in the woods, but I found that they have a liking for clover. Have you ever been walking in the woods and thought you heard a tractor starting? I did, and it was so strange, because I knew for a fact that where that noise was coming from there was nothing but alder brush and a small ridge with oak and maple on it. Very quietly, I made my way in that direction trying to be quiet. Going through alder brush is like trying to walk on broken glass without making any noise. Not saying it can't be done, but most people could not do it. They walk too fast and very seldom watch where they walk. Anyways, when I got to the edge of that ridge I heard the same noise and it was real close. One step at a time I made it maybe fifteen feet up the side of the ridge using the trees for cover and watching everything. There on a downed log were two partridge. One was stretching his neck out and beating his wings slow at first and then faster. That is called drumming and it does sound like an old tractor starting up. I stood there for a couple of minutes watching and looking around to see if it was calling in any more birds. When checking out the branches of the trees, I saw a large nest made of small branches and leaves. Cool, I thought to myself, gray squirrels. Well, why not? There were a few oaks on the ridge. I read if you find oaks that you might find grays. And in closer inspection I found several large nests up in the tree tops. Funny, I have been on this ridge many times in the past and never noticed them before.

One day I took a walk to one of my favorite places to sit and watch the wildlife we had living around us. It was early, but not real early, and the place I was going to was a waterhole that I found. On one side was a bog with a bunch of cedars that lined it. On the other side were small birches mixed with alder brush, and on both ends were pines. I would sit there for hours being very quiet. I had seen deer, bear, birds, and squirrels, all using the same watering hole. Not all at the same time, but throughout the day. So you really never knew what was going to show up.

On this day I am sitting, and I hear this noise . . . like something running. It was making a lot of racket. Then I see this rabbit come running like its tail was on fire! It ran right into this hollow log that was maybe a foot away from my feet. Then things were quiet, except for a slight rustling of leaves. I'm listening, trying to catch sight of what it was. It would move and stop, move and stop. Then just like magic, there was this big brush wolf . . . nose to the ground, heading straight for me! Great! Here I am, sitting on the ground . . . no gun, no knife, no nothing to defend myself with if things were to go bad. Anyway, I'm sitting there, and this wolf is getting closer and closer, and I'm getting a little nervous. The wolf stopped at the end of the log where the rabbit had run into just a minute or two ago. Now he is right at the end of my feet. He knew I was there, because he was staring me right in the eyes. I did not blink or move a muscle. I was just checking this guy out. What a good looking animal. I would have loved to have him for a pet. His coat was full and he had this long bushy tail. He was kind of brownish in color. After a second, he put his face down at the opening of the log and was growling a little. Then he started using his front paws to try to dig the log up or break it or whatever. Then he jumped up in the air and landed on the log and that was all it took. That rabbit shot out of that log like a flash! But he was just not fast enough! That wolf had him pinned to the ground and had grabbed him right by the head. The squeal that rabbit made had my hair standing on end! Couple of quick shakes of the wolf's head and the rabbit was still. Then the wolf turned, looked at me, raised his lips so I could see his teeth, and then disappeared into the woods from wherever he came from, taking his catch with him. Where is a camera when you want one? I would have loved to have that whole thing on film. Surprising enough, I really was not scared. After all, he never threatened me, he was just getting his meal. I sat for awhile longer and went home. When I got there, my step-father was in a lawn chair grilling some food on an outdoor grill he had made. I told him what had just happened and all he said was that I was not to go in the woods unless I had a gun or something to protect myself with. Ok, after that I took his advice. Things could have gone the other way and I would have been in a world of hurt.

Chapter 3

Opening day of small game and it was a little overcast and very windy. But the weather never really mattered much. I got dressed in my camo clothes. They didn't match, but that was just fine with me. It seemed that because of that it broke up my outline just that much more. Besides, I really had no choice in the matter. I had gotten all of my hunting clothes from rummage sales that my mother and I had stopped at on the occasional weekend trip to town. When we did stop at one, the first thing I would look for was hunting and fishing stuff. Every once in awhile I would hit the jackpot, and there would be deer calls or fishing plugs, camo boots, hats, gloves, jackets, ect. My mom would look for pants, shirts, winter coats, ect. We never had a lot of money to buy things, but we always managed.

Anyway, back to opening day. Because I had spent so much time in the woods, I knew more than likely where the animals would be held up on rainy, windy days. I would hunt the pines where there was good cover for them and a good place for them to perch. On a good day, no wind or very little wind, I would hunt the trails where they would be feeding or getting gravel. When I say they, I'm referring to partridge. And if I could not flush any partridge, I would keep an eye out for squirrels [grays] or rabbits. I would put a few miles on because each one of these animals lived in a different part of the woods. Depending on what they ate, what kind of cover they had, and access to water. Three things that no matter what you hunt, you have to think about if you want to get what you're after. Well, today I decided to be stubborn and concentrate on partridge. It was very slow, I had not seen or heard anything. I had searched several patches of pines with no results. This all takes time to do correctly and I was running out of time. So, I cut across country to a couple of gravel pits that I knew of that had pine and cedar trees along the edges. Within the first few minutes after getting there, I had shot my first partridge of the season. Now, no matter what, today was a success.

I quickly field dressed my bird, which is easy to do. You don't need anything to do this with. You simply put the bird on the ground, spread out its wings, put both your feet on them, grab the legs, and pull straight up. What you end up with is a very nice breast and wings. You wrap up the breast with the wings and put them in your pouch or pocket, and your hands are free to hunt some more.

By the time I had covered the gravel pits it was time to head back home with the three birds I had shot. I had a very good day.

The next day, Sunday, I got up, went outside, and was greeted by a beautiful sunny day. The wind had slowed down and I decided to go hunt that oak ridge that I had mentioned earlier. It was still early by the time I had reached the ridge, so, I thought I'd kill some time and just find a spot to sit and see just what was on this ridge. I already knew of the grays and I had seen a couple partridge, but sometimes it's just a good thing to sit, watch, and listen. After all, I had all day, and was in no hurry to go home. If there were any partridge on that ridge, I didn't see or hear them. I thought I had been quiet going through the alder brush getting to the ridge and picking out a good place to sit.

After several minutes of sitting down, I was looking up at the tree tops. I noticed in the notch of a large oak branch a pair of tiny, furry ears and right below them were a tiny pair of eyes not moving but just looking straight at me. That's when I knew that for as quiet as I was, that this squirrel had heard me and was checking me out. I just sat very still watching that gray. A short time later the gray disappeared. Then I started hearing leaves rustling around on the ground and figured that the gray had climbed down the tree and was going about his business. Except I was hearing leaves rustling in several different places on the ridge. Then I started seeing grays all over the place, not to mention a couple of them running through the tree tops. I was watching them run up and down the trees and you could hear their tiny feet grabbing the side of the trees with their claws. You could hear them talk to each other by what you could only call a 'barking' sound. You could see them going through the upper branches, knocking down acorns, then running down the tree finding them, and burying them in the leaves. There were way more grays here than I had thought. Then I heard one barking like crazy and it was like everything went quiet. The grays I had been watching simply disappeared.

Then I heard what I thought was a gray heading my way. The leaves would rustle then stop, then rustle some more, and stop. It was a couple of does who had come there to eat the acorns that the grays had knocked down. So the deer were using this ridge also! But they did what the grays didn't do. They must have scented me, for as soon as they got down wind of me, their tails went up and they were gone. Again, things were quiet. Then like before, the grays came back out and continued doing what they were doing before the deer showed.

I had spent enough time there and decided I was going to look for some birds. I got up very quiet just to see how close I could get to these woods rats. So I would not spook them, I would take a couple steps, stop, then take a couple steps, then stop. I heard the warning bark from one of the grays and everything was quiet. One of them had spotted me. I'm passing an oak tree, not seeing anything, but I heard this scratching sound coming from the tree I was next to. I walked around the tree to see if it was a gray, but nothing. I stood still, took of my hat, and tossed it to the other side of the tree. When I did that, this big, bushy gray came around the tree and stopped. It saw me standing there, barked, and ran up the tree and was gone. I just figured out another way of hunting grays. Any one that thinks that squirrel hunting is easy never tried to sneak into their house without being seen. It was written in an outdoor magazine I read once that they are just as hard to hunt as deer, and I believe it.

I spent the rest of the day walking trails bird hunting and managed to bag a couple partridge before returning home. That night we had a partridge dinner. My step-father was a heck of a cook. This man had a way of making everything come out tasting great.

My step-dad had a .22 semi-auto tube fed. The following weekend I asked him if I could use it. He asked me why, since I had a shot gun? I told him that I wanted to go after some grays and the shotgun tore them up too much. He agreed, but said that I had to replace whatever shells I used. That was fair. After all, the shells were not free, and I did make some money selling night crawlers.

I had a sign that I put up at the end of the drive way [night crawlers, 50cents a dozen]. I never sold a lot, but I did sell some. And they were free, I just had to go out at night and pick them out of the garden. I'm thinking maybe there was a reason that he showed me how to catch them.

Saturday morning I got out of bed and looked outside. It looked like a nice day for hunting grays. I put on my camo shirt and pants, grabbed my camo hat, ate breakfast, and did the few chores that I had to do. Then I went and found an empty cardboard box, grabbed a black marker, and drew a couple of circles on the side of the box. I went and asked my step-father for his .22 rifle. He took it from his room and handed it to me along with a box of shells. I pointed the barrel at the floor and took it outside. He always stressed gun safety. He said that if I didn't handle a gun the correct way, I would not be allowed to handle one at all. The target I had just made was already outside. I picked it up and carried it along with the .22 out behind the garage. I laid down the rifle, grabbed the target, and walked off about 30 steps, which was just about 60 feet. I faced the circles towards the garage and walked back to where I had set the rifle down. I looked at the target to make sure that it was in a safe place. There were no houses, just field and a slight downhill slope, so when I fired, the bullets would go into the ground. I sat down and checked to make sure the safety was on, pulled the rod out of the tube, and loaded the rifle. I replaced the rod in the tube, put the rifle to my shoulder, and looked down the sights at the target. When I felt comfortable, I took the safety off, took a small breath, and fired a round at the target. Without removing the rifle from my shoulder, I took another short breath, let it out, and fired a second round at the target. Then removing it from my shoulder, I put the safety back on, set it down, got up, and walked back to the target I made. Both rounds had found there mark right where I had aimed. I was satisfied that if that had been a gray, it would be going home with me. I picked up the box, turned around, and started back to the rifle. There was my step-father with his .22 in his hands. "Just checking" he said to me. I knew he had checked to see that I had put the safety back on before setting it down. "Let's see" he says. I showed him the target with two holes next to each other in the center of the inside circle I had put on the box. "Nice shooting" he said, and he handed me the .22. He took the box from me, turned, and walked back to the house. Again I checked the safety to make sure it was on, and headed across the field to go hunt grays.

I knew exactly where I was going . . . straight to that oak ridge. I could have been there a lot earlier, but I wanted to make sure of where the rifle was hitting. The last thing I wanted to do was shoot a gray just to have it run off to suffer and die. I believe that you just don't shoot an animal if you don't plan on eating it, and to shoot so it doesn't suffer. That means taking your time and making sure that your first shot counts. Today, because I wanted to get to the oak ridge as quiet as possible, I decided on a different trail to take. Instead of going to the far corner of the field and straight in, I cut short and headed to the creek. Once I got there, I waded up the creek to where I could see the oak ridge. It meant getting my feet wet, but it saved me fighting my way through a lot of alder brush. This way I only had ten or fifteen feet of brush to sneak through. Before I got to the edge of the brush, I had stopped and just stood still, searching the hill in front of me for signs of life. I had managed to sneak up without disturbing the ridge. The grays were out and about, running around, doing what grays do best. Not too far in front of me were a couple large oaks. Without moving, I started scanning them for movement. Sure enough, about half way up, I spotted a tail. The rest of the body was hidden behind a bunch of leaves. I waited to see if it would move farther out on the branch, but it just sat there not moving. Maybe I could make him show himself. Looking down on the ground I spotted a small stick by my foot. Carefully, I slowly bent down and picked it up. Then, I looked to see if the gray was still there, and he was. I tossed the stick onto the ridge on the other side of the tree the gray was in. When it hit the ground it rustled a few leaves, and that was just enough. The gray I was watching turned completely around and was facing toward the direction the stick had landed. That was all I needed! I took the safety off, raised my rifle up to my shoulder, sighted in on the gray's head, and squeezed of a shot. He rolled off the branch and fell to the ground and did not move. From where I was, I could still see him. I decided not to move in and pick him up, he was not going any place. Instead, I started looking in the tree tops for another one. I knew that after the shot it would take awhile for them to settle down and resume what they were doing. Sure enough, a short time later, I again heard the rustling of leaves and spotted a second gray sneaking down the same tree that I had just shot his friend out of. This one was coming down head first, a little at a time, tail twitching. It's head was moving back and forth listening for any sound. I shouldered the .22 and again put the sights on the gray's head. I waited for it to stop and squeezed off another round. Just like before, it dropped to the ground and was still. This time I moved in. One step at a time, as quiet as possible, and very slowly. I reached the two grays, picked them both up, and headed along the edge of the ridge. I put them on the ground and sat with my back to another oak tree and waited again for things to settle down. This time things had changed. I think that the grays knew that something was up. There was no rustling of leaves, just a bark once in awhile.

I started still hunting my way across the ridge. Taking a few steps, then stopping, looking, and listening for movement. Then taking a few more steps, watching where I placed my feet so as not to step on any branches or dried twigs, anything that would make noise. While doing this I was also watching the tree tops and that's where I spotted my next gray. He had just jumped from one upper branch to another. If I did not know better, I would say that they could fly from tree to tree. They were actually running across the tree tops. This one was using the upper branches to circle around me. I kept an eye on him, just waiting for him to stop long enough for me to get him in my sights. And that's just what he did. When he got behind me he stopped on a small branch and was watching me. Big mistake! Number three.

I back tracked to pick him up. I had taken two or three steps, was passing a tree, and I heard a scraping sound and I knew just what it was. I stopped, took off my hat, tossed it to the other side of the tree I was passing, and poof, instant gray! He came around that tree in a flash. I was ready and waiting for just that. Number four!

I picked up my hat and grabbed the last two grays I had just shot. It was weird that these grays knew exactly where I was. I had just passed that tree. I hadn't seen anything or heard anything, but he was there. Do you ever get the feeling you are being watched but no one is there? I'm thinking that there were still several grays watching my every move, but holding up tight. I worked the rest of the ridge and had not spotted or heard anything else. Then I headed back to the creek to take care of the four I had just gotten. Once there, I pulled out a small pocket knife that I had bought at a rummage sale. A small, one bladed Old Henry, more than enough to do what I had to do. I was just finishing up cleaning out my last gray when I heard barking coming from the ridge. That was a good sign that there were at least a few more there. I would be back another day to hunt that ridge. I headed home and left the ridge in peace.

After I had gotten back home I finished cleaning out the grays, washing them up, and was going to put them in the freezer. My step-father was in the kitchen and told me to just leave them in the sink, he was going to cook them up while they were still fresh. He puts them in a batter he makes and deep fries them. They are so tasty. I was on my way outside to bury what was left of the grays in the garden and he reminded me to make sure that I saved the tails. He used them for making dry flies for fishing. Very little was ever wasted. I always thought what we got from the creek and the woods was a gift. That night as I sat outside cleaning the .22, which was a must after using it, I thought about the day on the ridge and how the grays lived there. How they watched out for each other. How they gathered food and stored it for later, the nests they made up in the tree tops, and how they ran across those tree tops. Simply put, they're an amazing little animal.

So the rest of the season went well. I had gotten my share of partridge, even though it seemed like there really were not that many this year. The squirrel hunting was great. I had found several different spots that held a lot of grays. I did not hunt any single spot out and they were able to regroup.

Chapter 4

Rabbits were totally different. I would hunt the cedar swamps, alder brush, and along the creek. During the winter there were rabbit trails all over these places and it looked like there would be lots of them around. I would put snares out for them along the trails and brush piles. For every ten snares I'd put out, I might get one or two snowshoe rabbits. Or I'd see where one had been, only to have a fox, wolf, or something eat it right on the spot, nothing left but hair and blood. This did not make me happy, so I just quit hunting them.

During the season I had put a lot of miles on in these woods following animal trails. Always looking at what was around me and the tracks on the trails . . . where they went and where they came from. Once in awhile I would even catch sight of what was using the trail I would be on. Most of the time it would turn out to be a deer trail. There were lots of deer. It was the perfect place for them, lots of cover, plenty of water, and more than enough food. Not only in the field, but along the creek and in the alder brush. Every deer season I would see a few of our neighbors hunting the woods behind our house. And every once in awhile I'd see them haul out a nice doe or two and maybe some six or eight point buck. They always hunted the same way every year. A couple of stands had been put up along the edge of the field where they would post a couple of people. Three or four of them would push the ridges and the walking trails out to them. It seemed to work for them.

After the season was over I would go out into the woods and see just how those deer would go right around them. The big bucks . . . I would see ten, twelve point bucks trailing some very large does. These deer, the older, smarter ones, were using the alder brush and creek bed to travel on. They knew that the people that hunted out there never went into that. I was not going to tell them anything about it. In a couple of years I knew that I would be out there deer hunting, it was just a matter of time. My step-father hunted deer, but he always went with his brothers and they hardly ever got anything. I'd ask him "why not just hunt out here"?, but he would always say "there are no deer out there". Even though he would see them just about every night out in the field. What? Were they just supposed to just disappear during deer hunting season? Yes, they do tend to be a little more cautious, but they never really go any place.

I'm thinking that my step father and his brothers spent most of the season in the bars and going hunting was just an excuse to get out of the house. There were lots of deer in those woods.

One time, in the late spring, I had been sitting in one of the tree stands that those other hunters had put up, and I was given a gift. I got to watch a doe give birth! How many people do you know that can truthfully say that? It was something I would always remember. Another time I watched two large bucks sparring. They were both ten point plus and I have never seen anyone drag one of those big bad boys out.

For the next few years I spent a lot of time watching those deer. Learning their habits, the things they would feed on, places where they would lay up according to what kind of weather we were having and what time of year it was.

During pre-rut I would find scrapes and tree rubs. During rut I have seen bucks do really crazy things that they would not otherwise do. Like, run right out in front of hunters and not even think about it. Or cross a large field right in the middle of the day. It got to be kind of a game after awhile, to see just how close I could get to them without spooking them. I had walked up close enough to slap one doe right on the back side. I found out that deer are like rabbits. If you spook one and it runs off, you can run after it. Sometimes the deer only runs a short way, stops, and turns to see what is chasing it. A couple times I have done that and actually ran within a couple of feet of them, and there you are, eyeball to eyeball. It's a little unnerving, but all you do is back slowly away, give them space, and they turn and walk away. Maybe after me following them around for years they got to know that I was not a threat?

Chapter 5

By this time my home life, which was always touch and go, had gotten to a point where I did not feel comfortable anymore. My step-father for as long as I knew him drank a lot, and when he did, he got mean. But he has really started to be very physical in the last few years. Not only to me, but with my mother. Well, I had a choice to stay at home and maybe be seriously hurt or leave. I left.

For the next four or five years I did very little hunting or fishing, if any. Not once did I forget about the time I had spent out in the woods, but I had just too many things to do just to be living on my own. And besides, I had met a nice looking girl. Things happened, and we had a lovely baby girl. Then it was really hard to find time to do all the things I wanted to do. We would go up to the local lakes fishing together, but it just was not the same. Granted, we ate a lot of fish. Whether in a lake or in a stream, fish are fish. Use the right bait for what time of year it was and find structure, and you will find the fish.

We lived in a town called Duluth. If you have ever been there, you would see a ship canal that allows the larger ships access to Lake Superior from the Saint Louis River. Well, the pier as I call it, was a fish factory. Every July through August it would be lined with people fishing from it. I just happened on that fact when one day I was going to Park Point and had to cross the canal

using the lift bridge. I was crossing and noticed a large group of people fishing there on the pier. So, me being me, stopped to go see just what they were catching. It was mostly older men fishing there. The pier itself was ten or twelve feet wide and had walls that were maybe two feet wide on both sides. From the top of the wall to the water line was just about eight feet. There were guys sitting on the walls with their long handled fishing nets along side of them. Their nets were large and I wondered just how big these fish were and what kind of fish they were. Well, as luck would have it, I had stopped next to this older man and started talking to him about what they were fishing for. He explained to me they were catching Northern Pike. When I say lucky for me, that old man and I became good friends and spent many, many hours fishing that pier.

Anyway, as we kept talking, I learned just what kind of gear I needed to fish there and what kind of bait I needed. As I was standing there talking to him, someone down the row of people grabbed his fishing rod and yanked it back so hard I thought his rod would break, but all it did was bend and the fight was on! Guys on either side would reel their lines in so they wouldn't get their lines crossed. Someone would grab a net and give a hand netting the fish, Like I said, the water line was eight feet below the top of the wall, so the person netting would have to lean over the wall to get the fish in the net. When the net came back over the wall there was a Northern Pike about eight-ten pounds. "Nice fish" I commented, and the old man I was talking to goes "yes", that it was "an average size fish". Average I'm thinking, this was huge! Then he explains to me that they have been getting them up to twenty one pounds! I knew that I would be spending some time down there fishing. Not only was it walking distance from where I was living but I was not catching fish that large over the hill in the smaller lakes. My wife, [yes, we got married shortly after my daughter was born] and I would still go up to those smaller lakes fishing, having picnics, whatever, but I knew where I wanted to be. It just was not a good place to take my daughter. There was no place for her to play and it got very hot down there.

As time went on I was spending more and more time at the pier. We were too young to get married or to have kids, but neither her nor I had thought about that. And as it turned out, we never really got along with each other and ended up separating. After we split up I really spent a lot of time there. Fishing and talking to "the old man of the pier", as I called him. We used heavy fiberglass rods, open faced reels, fifteen pound test line with two foot wire leaders, large hooks, and very large sucker minnows or smelt when we could get them. We would put a large minnow on and a bobber the size of an orange about six feet above that, cast it out as far as we could, then just wait. There were days when you could catch those Northern one right after another. Sometimes you could cast out a fresh minnow and before your bobber had a chance to set on the water it would be going straight under with a fish on. We missed a few, but very few, and we released most of them. For myself, I was more into catching and releasing than I was in keeping to eat, after all, it was just me. A ten pound plus fish was more than enough for a couple meals, but I was fishing. Those Northern Pike stayed in there for a few years and the biggest I caught was an eighteen ponder. That day I was by myself and no net. I had to carefully walk down the wall, keeping the fish in the water so he would not spit the hook. Once at the end of the wall I jumped to the beach and landed my fish by hand. That one I kept. I brought it to a friend's house and we grilled it and fed a few of us. When the fish started to disappear, so did the fishermen. Then for a short time it seemed like the old man and I were the only ones left fishing down there. Then one day the old man just quit showing up. I wondered what was up and I was talking to a guy one day and he had told me that my friend had died. That was a bad day for me. I not only lost my fishing partner but I lost one of the very few friends I had. I still think of him and remember all the talks we had. He was like a father figure to me.

Chapter 6

Fishing the big lake, Lake Superior, has spoiled me totally, even though I fish it from shore. A person might not catch a lot of fish all the time, but usually when you do catch a fish, it's a nice one. Just like any other lake, it has its special times when certain fish come in closer to shore, depending on what time of year it is. Like in the spring when the rivers empty the winter runoff into the lake, and the Steelhead Trout go up the rivers to spawn and the Loppers are still in the shallows. The Walleyes are headed up the Saint Louis River to spawn and are only around for a few weeks. And the smelt run that attracts a lot of people every year. Not to mention the small Coho and Jack Salmon that travel the shallows. Summer, when the Northern and Musky are in close, feeding on the smaller fish when the water warms up. In the fall Lakers and King Salmon make their shot at the rivers and are close enough to fish from shore. Finally winter, but because of the size of the lake, it does not freeze totally. Not saying it hasn't, because once about every seven or eight years it has. Normally though, you have to wait for the pack ice to come in from the main part of the lake. Ice fishing the big lake is not for the weak of heart. You have a lot of things to watch out for. You have to watch the wind to see which way it's blowing. The last thing you want is to be stuck on the ice pack that has broken off and the next thing you know you are heading for Michigan!

When you do have the perfect day and the wind is blowing into shore, the ice is still never safe. Most of the time it's only a few inches thick and the ice rolls with the waves. Or pressure ridges form. It's always moving. But on those good days when you can get out, the fishing can be exciting. You can lay on the ice, look through the holes you have put in, and see five-ten feet down.

You can see schools of Herring or the occasional King traveling just under the ice. And if you do catch a fish, you can see it as you're reeling it in. Fishing Lakers in a hundred feet of water is not uncommon. I was fishing Lakers one time just off the pumping station. I was out about a half mile, maybe three quarters, fishing Lakers in one hundred and sixty feet of water on three inches of ice. Using thirty pound braded nylon line with a twenty pound mano leader and using an ounce and a half yellow lead head jig tipped with herring. The braded nylon was important when fishing that deep. Less stretch when setting the hook and you can feel the jig better when it hits the bottom.

You put your jig right on the bottom, then bring it up about a foot, then start jigging it maybe another foot from there. While jigging, if for any reason it feels like it stops, set your hook. I had caught several nice Lakers that day, the limit was three. If you like excitement, you just have to try this. But be aware of everything that is going on around you.

Chapter 7

I met my second wife who had a couple kids of her own when we got together. When we first got together she acted like she enjoyed doing the same things that I enjoyed. We would go out fishing with the kids to some of the trout lakes that were in that book that was given to me many years earlier. We also went to few of the smaller lakes and once in awhile the Saint Louis River. It was a good place to take the kids, there was always something there that would bite on their bait. I even went as far as to play hooky with the kids on a nice day just to take them fishing. It was just something I enjoyed doing with them. The way I looked at it was they were still in elementary school and missing one day was not going to ruin their education, but I might give them something to remember for the rest of their lives.

Work was spotty, six months here, a year there. I always worked, just no place long term. I had gotten back into hunting. The way I saw it is that it was helping feed my family.

This guy I met, who ended up being my hunting partner for many, many years, felt the same way as I did about feeding his family wild game. He was married and also had a couple kids, so whatever we got hunting was never wasted. We would hunt squirrels, partridge, bear, deer . . . if it moved and was good to eat, we would hunt it. We taught each other a lot about hunting, what I was not too sure of, he was. We fished some, but not a whole lot. He liked the smaller inland lakes and I liked fishing the big lake. He fished from his boat, he had a really nice boat. But the only thing I could never understand was, people go out and spend thousands of dollars on a boat, motor, and trailer, just to fish by the shore lines. I used to tease him a lot about that. Not always, but most of the time, I would catch more and bigger fish from shore than he did from his boat. Maybe that was another reason we did not fish much together.

We went duck hunting for a couple of years. That man was a duck slayer! It was something he excelled at. Myself, I really didn't care much for the taste of duck and gave up hunting them. I still held fast to my motto if you are not going to eat it, you just don't hunt it.

Anyway, it took awhile, but the kids lost interest in fishing and so did their mother. They had their friends and liked to hang out and do things with them. That was ok, it just meant that again I was more or less by myself, free to do the things that I enjoyed.

Chapter 8

During the summer months when fishing on the big lake was slow, I would still go out in the woods for a couple of reasons. As always, I would be out checking for deer sign. I would put on many miles looking in different areas where there was open state land so before opening day of deer season I already knew where I was going to be hunting and had a good idea of the land I was going to be hunting on, a good idea of where the deer were, their bedding areas and feeding spots. I would be looking for natural tree stands by their trails. By that I mean trees that were big enough for me to sit in or spots on the top of a ridge that overlooked a cedar swamp that during season might hold deer looking for cover or a place to hold up during the day. Sometimes I would find an old tree stand that someone else had put up and abandoned for one reason or another. After I found a spot I wanted to hunt, I would mark the trail that I used, so that on opening morning I could get to my stand while it was still dark and not have to use a light. I would clean the trail of sticks that might snap or dead brush that would make a lot of noise going through. Season always started a half hour before sunrise and ended a half hour after sunset. Pre-season scouting was a must if you really wanted to have a good chance at getting a deer during season. The second was I had gotten into making diamond willow canes.

You might find an area with a hundred willow trees but there would only be one or two that would make a good looking cane. It would take a good year to make a cane. Finding just the right one was the easy part. Then you had to peel the bark off, carve off the parts that you did not want, and let it dry. That took about six months. Then you have to sand it down and that was time consuming. First you would start off with a coarse sandpaper and gradually work your way to a really fine sandpaper. That would bring out all the beautiful wood grain that made them look so good. Then you put the clear poly on, one coat

at a time. Two or three coats were more than enough. Sometimes I would have three or four of these canes going at the same time.

It was something to pass the winter hours when you couldn't get out ice fishing, and the money I would get for them would pay for hunting gear or a hunting or fishing license. After awhile, the wild game that I would bring home the family would no longer want to eat, so I was very limited to what I could take. My seasons were very short. Talking to my hunting partner about this we decided that we would talk to a few other people we knew about deer hunting and soon we had a hunting party of seven. When deer hunting, a person was able to shoot more than one deer as long as there was a person in the party who had an open tag and was hunting in the same area as you. Usually, the first week everyone more or less hunted for themselves. But by the second week, if there were tags that still were not filled, then we would get together and see if anyone wanted help in filling their tag. With seven of us hunting there were always tags that needed help being filled. Everyone wanted to fill their tag, that meant meat in their freezer, food on their table. This worked out good for my hunting partner and myself. Not to say that we were some kind of super hunters or anything like that, but both he and I would put in our time pre season scouting and we had a better understanding of the animal we were hunting. Some people have these dreams of seeing this great big buck with a huge rack just walking through the woods without a care in the world and that all they have to do is just walk out there and shoot him. Sorry, but that just don't happen. Sure, every once in awhile someone's stars are in order or lady luck is sitting with them, or whatever, and they do get a nice buck completely by accident. Like I say, bucks in rut do stupid things.

Or there are the bait hunters. The ones that have hunting shacks that are better looking than their houses. The ones who watch TVs, sit in their long johns and play cards all day. Who put piles of cracked corn or bales of clover fifty to a hundred yards from their shacks so all they have to do is look out a window to see if anything has come in to eat, open the window, and shoot their deer right in the bait pile. If this upsets you, sorry, but you know who you are. You would think that a person would have more respect for the animal. That is not hunting. You might as well just tie a deer up with a rope and shoot it. Thankfully, there are very few that do this, and most of the hunters I have come across are true hunters.

Anyway, our party of seven seldom would have a tag empty at the end of season. There were years where I would fill four or five tags myself, counting my own. Granted, most were does, but we would get a few nice bucks also. This might seem bad, but it really helped the deer herds in the long run.

There were people who I have met that knew of our party of seven and that we were most always pulling deer out, and they referred to us as 'meat hunters'. Well, we were meat hunters. We were out there to enjoy the hunt and put food on our tables. None of us were wealthy and just went out to trophy hunt. Please don't take this wrong, I would not mind having a nice twelve or fourteen point trophy buck on my wall. They are far and few between. Mostly on ranches where they are allowed to grow that big and fed special diets that help their antlers get that big. We all respected the deer we hunted for being the smart, beautiful animal they are. There is nothing easy about real hunting. Deer are very smart. For every one you see, at least a few have seen you, or scented you, or heard you, and you never see them. While sitting on a stand I have watched two hunters walking through the woods hunting only to pass right by a doe who simply laid down and waited for them to pass by. And I have watched a buck push a doe out of cover and wait to see if it was safe to come out. The bigger, smarter bucks, after hearing the first few shots of season, will run for cover and start only coming out after dark. That's how some get to be so big.

Then the hard part starts. It is taking care of the animal you have just harvested. The cleaning out, taking care that you don't contaminate the meat. Depending on how far out in the woods you hunt, it's the dragging of the animal back out to your car or truck. Taking it to be registered. Then hanging your animal some place cool to let it age, where no other animal is going to try eating it. For myself, I never let my deer hang over night. I would get it home, strip the hide off, and wash it down real good, getting the blood and hair off of it. Then butcher it and wrapping the meat. I would have it in the freezer by morning. The hide I would donate to Hides for Habitat and the bones and anything else that was not usable, would be double bagged and put out for the trash man to take away. Unless he had just been there, then I would freeze their remains and be sure to put them out on the morning when he would be there. Personally, I would rather take the time and bring what was left back out in the woods and leave it there. Between the birds, squirrels, and meat eating animals in the woods, nothing goes to waste. They have to survive too. In the landfill, I feel it is just a waste.

Have you ever heard of horror stories of all the deer every year that are dumped in our landfills because some hunter had not taken care of their deer and they think nothing of it? They just go out and do it again the next year. Should those people even be allowed to hunt? Or what about the hunter who sees a deer running across an open field, picks up his rifle, and empties a full clip at a running deer at over two hundred yards? Not thinking that there might be a house or a road or a bus full of kids going to school behind that running deer. Then not even getting out of his stand because the animal did not drop, to go see if he had even hit it. He just might have, and the animal runs off some place to die. The hunter tells his buddies about the thirty point buck he missed.

Believe me when I say that I am not anti hunting. I have hunted and shot many deer, but always, always was sure of my target and I had never had to make more than one shot. We as hunters have a responsibility not only to ourselves, but to others as well, and to the wild game we hunt. We need to know the area we hunt in. Where the houses are and where the roads are. Bullets travel long distances and whether you are shot at a foot or at five miles away, you are still shot. I am a firm believer in hunter safety classes. They do a great job. I just don't think it is enough. You listen to the news and every year there is someone dying in a hunting related accident and almost all of them could have been avoided.

The man or woman shot while in a deer stand dressed in full blaze orange, eight feet in the air, because some hunter shot at a deer that was on the side of a ridge. His rifle was not properly sighted in and maybe there was brush or trees in the way and he did not see the other hunter. Or the hunter who shoots his or her hunting partner because they trip. Their rifle is not on safety, it hits the ground and goes off, shooting the person in front of them. And the one who says, "I thought it wasn't loaded" and didn't think to make sure it wasn't loaded.

For a person to point a rifle or any weapon towards, or even in the same direction as someone else, loaded or not loaded, should never be allowed to put their hands on one. All of these accidents could have been avoided, but it happens every year. It not only destroys the lives of the person shot, but destroys the life of the person who, with a little bit more care, could have avoided the accident.

Chapter 9

Too many other things can happen during hunting. Like what happened to me one year. A co-worker and I were talking about deer hunting and he suggested that I come hunt his property sometime. He said he had several large bucks running around his place and that he had a nice stand by the edge of this field that I could hunt out of. I agreed and we made plans for me to come out the following weekend. I told him that I liked to get in my stand before sunrise and just sit and wait. He said that he didn't have a problem with that. There was a wide trail that lead directly to the stand and that I would have no problem finding it. He had it set up very nice and was correct, I did not have a problem finding the stand. For some reason or other, the deer that morning must have been hanging out somewhere else. I sat in that stand from sunrise until noon and never saw a thing. A beautiful sunrise and a couple fox playing in the field, but no deer. So I decided to get down and get some coffee from my truck and stretch my legs. On the way back to my truck I was thinking of this other spot I knew of and maybe I should just go hunt there for a couple hours. After I put my gear away, I went and knocked on the door to let him know that I was heading someplace else and to thank him for letting me hunt his property. No one was home, so I wrote a note letting him know what I was doing and thanked him. I put it on his front door and left.

This other place I was going just happened to be at my parent's place. Where I grew up and first started hunting. I knew the area well and had a good idea where the deer would be at that time of day. The sun was shining and it was a warm day for this time of year. I parked the truck in the driveway and went into the house. No one was home, so I left my mother a note telling her that I was out in the woods deer hunting and just about where I was going to be at. She lived there by herself now, my step-father had died a year earlier.

I pulled my gear out and headed for the corner of the field where I knew of a huge white pine that I had sat in many times in the past. It sat in such a place that once in it, I could not only see the field but a ridge that surrounded the field. Plus, I could look down into a large alder brush area that was full of deer trails. When I got to the pine, like I had done many times in the past, I unloaded my rifle. Because I always used a sling, put my rifle on my back and up I went. There were large branches that I used like a ladder and soon was sitting in my favorite place. There were three large branches that made a perfect seat. I then took my rifle, loaded it, and got comfortable. Soon I saw a couple of does walking through the alder brush. I was high enough that they did not see me or scent me. I decided to just let them walk, satisfied to just watch them feed and slowly move out of sight. By then a breeze had picked up and hearing anything was hard to do. I was standing up, stretching my legs, and watching the field. Like magic, about seventy five yards away, I spotted movement heading in my direction. I wasn't sure what it was. A buck or maybe one of the does I had seen earlier? I kept watching, it seemed like it took forever, and whatever it was must have gone in another direction. I turned to look behind me, then turned back, to see a nice buck standing half way up on the ridge with his nose stuck up in an overhanging pine branch. I knew he was laying a scent trail for other deer to follow and he more than likely had a ground scrape directly below that branch. First thing

I did was start counting points. A little hard to get a good count because his head was up in the pine branch, but I managed to count at least ten points. After that I decided, ok, I was going to take this buck. He was only fifty yards away, standing broad side. Perfect! The rifle I was using was a 30.06 single shot, bolt action, with a four power scope. My weapon of choice. I put the cross hairs on where I knew his heart was and squeezed off a shot. The buck dropped right there. It never took a step, but I put another shell in the chamber and waited for a couple of minutes, just in case he would get up and try to make good an escape. Besides, I also wanted to settle down. Even though I have shot a lot of deer, I still get excited. When I felt sure that he was not going anywhere I unloaded my rifle, put it on my back using my sling, turned to climb down the way I came up . . . and that's when my world fell apart! The branch I had been standing on, which was big enough and strong enough to build a house on, snapped! The next thing I knew I had fallen about eight feet and landed on a lower branch. I was draped over this branch like a sheet on a clothes line. The wind was knocked out of me and I felt a sharp pain in my chest. I could see that I was still some ten feet off the ground. I just hung there, trying to pull myself together enough to finish climbing down. Once back on the ground I assessed the damage I had just caused myself and rested for a bit. It was a good thing that my rifle was on a sling and strapped to my back. Who knows what would have happened to it if it had been knocked out of my hands. As far as I could tell I had only bruised a rib or two. It hurt like crazy to breathe, but I was not bleeding. So I took my rifle off my back, loaded a shell into the chamber, and put the safety on. Then I headed to where my buck should be laying. He was right where I had shot him, he had died instantly. From up in the tree I knew he was a good buck, but standing next to him was a totally different story. I grabbed his rack and tilted his head back to get a good look at him. I started counting points. There was a total of twenty one points, including a drop tine. Legally there were only sixteen that were over one inch long, so I had just shot a nice sixteen point buck. Having shot and weighed many deer, I was looking at a two hundred plus deer.

Now I had a lot to do. I dug out of my pockets the two knives I carry just for this reason. I use them for field dressing only because they hold a near perfect edge. Field dressing a deer will dull most knives in a heart beat and a dull knife is a dangerous knife.

With that done, I started looking for the best possible course to take to get this buck up the ridge and into the field above. Still hurting a lot from my trip down from the tree, I knew that I was in for a very long, hard drag back to my truck and it was already two thirty and it was getting dark by five. From another one of my pockets I took out eight feet of nylon rope. Cargo pants have very large pockets and I carry a lot of things in them. So, unloading and putting my rifle on my back again, I tied one end of the rope around his rack and started moving him a couple of feet at a time up the ridge. Little did I know how steep it was until I started dragging a large deer up it. It was hard with all the brush, trees, stumps, and large rocks thrown down when they first cleared the field for haying many years ago. Finally reaching the edge of the field, which was a chore, exhausted, sweating like crazy, and in a lot of pain. Again I took a break, looking at the house far off in the distance and thinking how just that one accident could have seriously injured me or even killed me. Strange how things just happen and I still had a long way to go. Again, like the ridge, I just did not think that it was so far across the field and back to the house. It was dark by the time I had gotten half way across and I'm starting to get a little worried. There was a lot of howling going on behind me from the direction I had just came from. I'm sure that a bunch of coyotes or brush wolves had found the remains of this deer. If the field had not been turned over lately I would have just driven my truck to the deer, but without four wheel drive, it was not a good thing to try. By the time I reached the truck it was almost seven pm, a very long day. Putting my gear in the truck, the deer in the back, and leaving my mother a note . . . she had been home but went out to bingo, I then headed to register my deer and have it weighed. It came out field dressed at two hundred forty one pounds, the biggest deer I had ever shot.

On the way home I'm wondering where I'm going to put this buck. There was just no way I was going to be able to do anything that night. I decided to just hang it in the basement where it was cool until the following morning. When I got back to the house the kids were sleeping, so I brought the deer into the basement and hung it up. I put papers on the floor to keep it from getting too messed up. My wife had come downstairs and was not too thrilled with the idea of a deer hanging in the basement and was very vocal about it. So I explained that I would take care of it the next day because I had injured myself while out hunting and was just too tired to do it that night, Thinking back now, the handwriting was on the wall, that it was not going to be long after that we would separate.

Chapter 10

Practice, practice, practice. Whether you hunt with a rifle or a bow or a slingshot. Whatever you hunt with, the key word is practice. Know your limitations. I could fill pages with deer hunts that I have done, but won't. This next section is about deer hunting, but with a bow.

For years I hunted strictly rifle. A person that worked with me was an avid bow hunter and asked me if I had ever tried it. No, can't say as I had, but somehow or other he had talked me into getting a bow. There is a lot of respect to be had for bow hunting. Not only do you have to get up close and personal, but you need the upper body strength to be able to be at full draw and hold until your shot is there.

The Matthews bow I picked out was good enough for me. For the first year all I did was practice. At first it was once a week, then two or three times a week. At first it was set at fifty pounds. By the end of the first year I was pulling and holding seventy pounds, could group three or four arrows in the center at thirty to forty yards. Well, that was ok. It was not that hard to get within that distance when all camoed out. Many times in the past I have gotten that close and closer. With the right wind, watching where you walk, using the natural cover around you to conceal your movements. It's called still hunting and with practice anyone can get good at it.

I was using carbon arrows for a faster shot and instead of sighting pins, there was a cross hair type front sight and Muzzy broad heads. My very first deer hunt with a bow turned out to be my best. Granted, the buck that I shot was only a six pointer, but the excitement was so great you would have thought it was my very first deer. Shot from a stand where there was deer sign all over the place in front of me. After sitting for half the day and not seeing anything at all, there was a rustling of leaves like a squirrel or some small animal running around behind me. Slowly turning just my head to see what was there, I spotted this six point buck standing still next to a group of cedar trees. I could see his head and his tail, that was it. Turning my head back behind the tree that held my portable stand and standing up so I could get my bow ready. Knocking an arrow, setting my release, then turning. Trying to be quiet and stay out of sight to hide any movement, I looked back around the tree. The deer had moved just a little, now only showing the front shoulder and rear quarter. Ok, that was good. Drawing back, setting my cross hairs just a little bit behind the front quarter and trying to hold steady for one well placed shot, I pulled the trigger on my release. I heard two sounds, my bow, and what sounded like someone hitting a tree with a log. The deer jumped like his feet were spring loaded and was gone in a flash.

Standing there I could hear him run off through the brush. I gave the deer time to lay up and bleed out for what seemed like a long time. I got down from my stand and walked over to where the deer was standing. It was a good thirty three yards. Looking for blood sign was not hard, there was plenty of it, along with my arrow. It had gone straight through the deer. Knowing in what direction he ran off was good, but not necessary. There was a good blood trail, and within fifteen yards I was looking at my first buck with a bow. The next couple of seasons were by bow. I had gotten a few does and one eight point buck.

There was a down side to bow hunting. The kills were not instant. A person had to track his deer, which meant the animal had suffered. This did not sit well with me. I quit hunting with a bow when one season I shot a large doe that I had watched walk about fifteen yards. The shot should have dropped the deer in its tracks, it was well placed. When the deer took off after the shot I could see the arrow sticking out of both sides of the doe, if nothing else it should have been a double lung shot. But after two days of trying to find this deer, I couldn't. It was then I promised myself that never again would I do that. The bow went up for sale and haven't touched one since.

This is not to say that everyone is like me. There are a lot of excellent bow hunters who have the right equipment, who practice, and know their bow inside and out. The ones that at forty or fifty yards can put a group of arrows into a spot no bigger than a poker chip consistently. I have a lot of respect for these people. To them I would be considered a beginner. Still, I did the best that I could do with the equipment that I could afford.

Chapter 11

My hunting partner and I had a place that we hunted bear. It was some land that his brother owned. It was way out in the country in the middle of nowhere. On one side of this trail that split his land was alder brush pines and swamp. On the other were hills covered with oaks and maples, one of our favorite places to hunt grays. Like most people, we had stands set up on trails and used bait piles to help bring in bear. We used nothing but vegetables. We found out that it worked out better that way. It was better than putting meat scraps in the pile that ended up rotting and smelling very bad.

We both would apply for and get our bear licenses. We did very good there, both getting our bear.

One season we were out bear hunting and after sitting in our stands all morning from sunrise to mid afternoon, we decided to get down and go grab something to eat, get some coffee, and so we could stretch our legs. Going back out to where we had parked my truck, we grabbed our lunch and thermoses and headed up the hill into the oaks and maples. That way we could eat our lunch and at the same time watch to see what the squirrels were doing. There were a lot of them on this hill, and every once in a while we might even see a deer or two cruising through there eating what the squirrels would knock down.

On that afternoon, the squirrels were being very busy. The acorn crop that year must have been really good, it sounded like rain out there. While we sat on the side of this hill we could see them running around, chasing each other, and hiding nuts under the leaves. It was very noisy. My friend tapped me on the shoulder and pointed across a small gully and up on the next hill. Looking closely, there was what at first looked like a large rock or a brush pile, then it started moving. It was still too far away to see it clearly, but it was heading down the hill. About half way down the hill it was clear to both of us what we were watching. It was a fairly large bear nosing around in the leaves for acorns. We watched him for about an hour. He never left the hill he was feeding on. Slowly, he did work his way back up the hill, and he was gone. My friend and I sat there for a little while longer, talking about what we had just seen and hoping that maybe that same bear would come over to the bait pile around dusk.

We left, went back to the truck, put our thermoses away, and went back to our stands to sit until dark, hoping that the bear we had seen earlier would show up. No such luck. We sat there the rest of the day and nothing at all came in. We both got down, went back to the truck and headed back to town. On the way, we were talking again about that bear. We decided that we would camo out and hunt that hill the next day and leave our stands empty. The next morning when I was getting ready and putting my stuff in my truck, I noticed that I had no shells for my rifle. When I unloaded the day before and put them in the box, somehow or other, I must have dropped them on the ground. Thinking to myself now, what was I going to do? I didn't have the money to go buy another box. Then I thought about my shotgun and went and looked to see what kind of shells I had for that. Lucky enough, I had three twenty gauge slugs. I had bought them a couple of years earlier for shotgun deer season and had only used two of them. I grabbed them and my shotgun and headed to go pick up my hunting partner. In the truck on the way to his brother's house, I was explaining why I was late picking him up. "Not a problem" he goes "crap happens".

When we got to his brother's it was still dark, so we were going to have some coffee and wait a little. We got out of the truck and went into the box. He grabbed his thermos and I went to grab mine and as soon as I did, in my mind I was picturing it sitting on the kitchen table. What else could go wrong today? My friend laughed at me saying what an air head I was and offered me some of his coffee. While we were drinking our coffee, I was walking around the back of the truck and I stepped on something, looked down on the ground, and guess what! There was my box of rifle shells. Well, that was good, except . . . my rifle . . . was at home, because I really did not expect to find them. And what was my friend, my hunting partner, doing? He was shaking his head and laughing so hard I thought he was going to bust a gut. And really, the only thing I could do was laugh with him. After all, isn't that just the way things happen?

We finished getting our camo gear on and my friend was looking at my shotgun and made the comment that he thought the camo job I had done on it was cool. I explained to him that I had found a store that had a rolls of como tape, that way when I got camoed out, the only thing on me that was not como was my face. We locked up the truck and headed up the trail to the hill. We entered the woods about three hundred yards apart. We hunted together so much we both knew all the time what the other one was doing. When I hit the top of a ridge, looking down, there was my friend. We hand signed that we would take a break and sit. I went down the hill to where my friend was and we sat there for awhile, being very quiet.

Like the day before, the squirrels were very busy, so it was kind of noisy. After a while, we agreed that we would go up the hill to a flat spot that we knew of. First, I would skirt the bottom of this ridge for a hundred yards and we would work the hill up together. Still hunting is so slow, but if you hope to see anything, that's what you have to do. Couple steps here, pause. Take a couple more steps, stop, check out the area. Just taking your time looking at everything.

We were both standing, just looking around, and an acorn hit me. I looked, and my friend was pointing at the very top of the hill. There was this bear, standing there, looking down the hill, right in our direction. A good looking black bear with this almost perfect white heart shape on its chest. We were both standing behind trees when he spotted him, so I don't think he saw us. But all at once he dropped to his rump, spun, and took off running. Over the hill and gone. He must have scented us, neither of us were moving. We just kept still hunting the hill. We get to the top and there is this flat spot. By now we were only about twenty yards apart. We stopped right at the top and coming in our direction was a second bear just entering the flat spot from the other side. This spot was maybe a little more than eighty yards wide and only a few trees in it.

We were standing there watching this black bear slowly heading in our direction and I mean directly at us. As it was getting closer, I could hear my friend whisper for me to take this bear out because I was closer than him. Ok, I said, but for me to get a good shot I had to let it get closer. My shotgun was a single shot and I wanted to make it count. I knew though, that if things went bad, my partner was right there. So as long as the bear was heading right to me, I'll just let him get as close as possible. This bear was close, may be twenty feet. My friend was getting excited. I could hear him whispering "shoot it, shoot it". I turned my head to see what he was going to do, turned my head back to the bear, and you might as well say he was right next to me. I could see the hair growing out of his eye lids. I already had my shotgun raised by my side pointed right him, so I just pushed it out to the side of his head, and pulled the trigger. When the smoke cleared, he was laying right there at my feet.

Surprisingly, I was completely calm while this all took place, but now my heart was going a hundred times a second. I looked up and my friend was already by my side with his rifle ready for a second shot if needed. It wasn't. That bear was not going anywhere. He had been up there eating acorns, because when I grabbed his head by an ear to look at him, a large bunch of chewed acorns come out his mouth. The twenty gauge slug had done its job and my partner's face was pale. He says "you are you completely crazy"! "Why didn't you shoot him before you did"? Just looking at him and smiling I said, "Why"? "He was coming right to me". He said that he was just about to pull the trigger. He was obviously quite shaken. By the time we had taken care of the bear, gutted it, and removed a canine tooth for DNR, he was back to his old self, laughing and joking around. We then drug it out and loaded into the back of the truck. I went to register it and my partner went and sat in his stand. When I got back he was on the trail waiting with a big smile on his face. "What's going on"? I asked him. He waited until I shut the truck off and got out before he said anything. Then he just asked me to follow him to his stand. When we got there, in the middle of one of the trails, laid the bear with the white heart on its chest. He said that he had just gotten into his stand and this bear came walking right in. By the time we got that bear loaded and registered it was dark. We hung both bears in his brother's garage, took off the hides, and left. We took care of the rest the next day.

I had met a guy once who told me that I didn't know what bear hunting was about until I hunted them on the ground and not from a stand. That guy knew exactly what he was talking about. It was totally an exciting experience. One that I know I will never forget and will do again. The tooth was sent to DNR and a couple months later I received a letter stating that the bear was a three year old. Amazing what they can tell from a tooth.

Chapter 12

Minnesota is full of wildlife and if a person was to want to spend a lifetime as a hunter, there is no better place to live. Out of all the big game animals that live there, the moose is the only one that I have not hunted. This is not to say that I did not want to or that I never had close encounters with them, because I have. It's just that I was never lucky enough to get a license to hunt them. Yes, I have applied for them, but it's on a lottery type system, once in a lifetime, but never lucky enough to get chosen for one.

I was on my way to go fishing one time up out of Ely, Minnesota. I was on my motorcycle going down the Wandless Trail, heading for a trout lake that had Splake and Brookies. Up ahead of me a large bull moose had walked out of the brush and onto the road. I stopped my bike and sat there, just looking at it. That moose was huge! The biggest one that I had ever seen and I have seen a few. His rack was large enough that I could have laid down in it and stretched out. Not knowing what he was up to, I had turned my bike around. So if he, for whatever reason, decided that he would come my way, I would be able to give him all the room that he wanted. A full grown moose is not an animal that you want to take lightly. I'm sure you have heard the stories of them turning over cars. And what about the one that charged a box car on a train, broke its neck, but derailed the box car. True or not I don't know, but I just would not doubt it. Anyway,

I had turned my bike and sat there watching him. He looked at me, lowered his head, and started in my direction. As he came my way I was going the other, keeping an eye on him. This only went on for a short distance. He stopped, turned his head, and looked the other way. Out of the brush where he had been, a cow, [female moose] came walking out, stopped, and looked in my direction. Then she headed down the road and into the brush on the other side of the road. No sooner than she had done that than the bull that had made me move, turned, and followed her. Too close for comfort! Then I went on my way fishing.

Another time I was out partridge hunting down a snowmobile trail. A nice sunny day, mid afternoon. Watching the trail up ahead of me I noticed a large, dark object on the side of the trail. From the distance I was, I just could not make out what I was looking at. Hunting birds, all I had was my twenty gauge shot gun with bird shot. I stopped and was trying hard to see what was up ahead of me. All of a sudden on my right side I heard a snort—like it was right in my ear! I froze, and the hair on the back of my neck stood up, and I got this shiver all the way up my back. I did not move a muscle. Then there was a second snort and at that I started moving backwards slowly. I took a couple of steps back and this great big cow came busting out of the brush right where I had been standing. As she came out she turned down the trail. When she did, I was bounced off the side of her. It did not knock me down, just back a few steps. Then as I watched her trot down the trail, it came real clear what I had been looking at. It had been a calf eating on the brush on the side of the trail. The two meet up and down the trail they went. I went home. That had been enough excitement for me for one day. I was very lucky that she did not just run me over and stomp me into the dirt. Thinking that being between a mother and her young was not a good place for any one to be.

This is my last close encounter with a moose. Early morning, opening day of deer hunting season. I was hunting alone, my hunting partner had to work. I was at a favorite spot we had hunted many times in the past. This was a small point of land covered in pine and brush. Bug Creek ran along one side of it and emptied into a small lake on the other. There were a couple of old tree stands on this point that someone had built before we ever started hunting here. I was headed for one of them, it was right along the side of a group of cedar trees.

After I parked my truck I got my gear ready. There had been a heavy frost the night before and I knew the ground was going to be crunchy. So, not wanting to make a bunch of noise, I put my boots around my neck and headed to the stand in my wool socks. It was working great, very little noise and I only had a half mile to go. Getting to the stand, I brushed off my socks, put my boots on, and got into my stand. This stand was only eight feet off the ground and no seat, so I had to stand there in the dark and wait for daylight. While I was waiting, there was the sound of something wading in the creek and the sound of things moving around in the brush. I knew that some buck had been bedding down on that point. I had run across his bedding area while doing my pre-season scouting. Another reason why I wanted to sneak in there. I wanted to catch him coming home or leaving his bedding area.

The sun had come up. There was little or no wind to mention and there was something still moving around in the brush. It would move and stop, then move and stop, and sounded like the noise was coming from several different locations. So, I'm thinking a buck and maybe a doe or two or a couple of bucks. The noise on one side of me was getting closer and closer. My rifle was ready and my heart was pounding, it always did when I heard an animal move into where I was. If you don't get excited when that happens you might as well quit hunting. The excitement is gone and that is a part of the hunt. So I'm really looking hard, searching every tree, every stand of brush. Looking for the twitch of an ear or a small patch of brown. A leg, anything that might be a deer sneaking by. Nothing, and the noise is still coming closer. Then I heard the breaking of what had to be a large branch coming from behind me. I turned to face the direction of the sound and started watching again. Nothing. I turned again to look in the direction of where the noises had been coming from before and to my surprise there were two moose. A cow and a calf standing side by side, with just their heads showing from around this cedar tree. Not moving, just standing there looking around. I had seen moose before up close and personal, but I had never seen one with a white face before, let alone two of them! They both had white faces. Then from behind I heard more brush moving real close. I'm thinking, since when do moose and deer hang out together? That thought cleared real fast. Moving right under my stand was a small bull moose. When I say small, I mean, he had a shovel rack. He just cleared the bottom of my stand. Then he stopped and just stood there for what seemed forever. He was right under my feet, just standing there looking at the cow and her calf. As quietly as they moved in, the cow and her calf started moving away from me. The bull waited for a bit and also started moving off in the same direction, just taking his time, not in any hurry. Again a heart thumping experience. Granted, this time I had a rifle with me and if things went wrong, I knew I had a chance of walking away. Thankfully it didn't. For the rest of the day I posted myself in that stand, until just before sunset and then headed out. It was dark before I got back to my truck and all the way home I thought about those moose. When I called my hunting partner that night to tell him about my day, he said he was not surprised because he had seen moose droppings back in there before. You just have to love hunting Minnesota, you never know what you will see.

Chapter 13

Let's get back to fishing. There are several places that I love to fish and I will mention them right now. First of them is a small, but well known trout lake located just out of Hill City, MN called Taylor Lake. My uncle took me to this lake for the first time when I was ten. My mother and I were visiting her mother, my grandmother, and my uncle asked me if I wanted to go fishing with him. I was excited and of course said yes. He had everything we needed to go and it was only about four miles from my grandmother's house. We loaded everything into a small trailer that he pulled behind a small tractor and off we went. About four miles down the road there was a white sand trail that went off to the right, up a small hill and back into the woods. About a quarter of a mile up the trail was this small lake and at the time was surrounded by brush and cattails. The only way you could fish it was to wade out into the lake. The bottom was mushy, but shallow. Then it got deep quick and there were only trout in it, Rainbow Trout. Because it was a designated trout lake you could not use minnows, just flies, leaches, and worms. We were using small bobbers, light line, and small hooks, casting out beyond the weeds and letting them float around. We caught and released a lot of trout that day, but my uncle did manage to catch and keep a three pound Rainbow, very nice fish.

Today, if you go to that same lake, it is completely different.

In an outdoor magazine quite a few years back, it was rated the first of ten best trout lakes in Minnesota. Today if you go there on opening day, it's so crowded that you can hardly find a place to fish. People come up a week early just to set up camp and wait. The fishing is that good. Everyone has a great time. There are camp sites all around the lake and plenty of fire wood cut and left by the forestry department. The edge of the lake has been all cleared of excess brush and a nice foot trail all around the lake. The woods surrounding the lake are covered with white lilies, maple, and oak trees.

Now there are Browns, Rainbows and Brookies. There is a nice place to put in canoes or a small row boat, and some people use float tubes. The whole lake is good fishing, but my favorite spots are to the right off where the trail hits the lake. Now I use four pound test, slip sinkers, and night crawlers. Taking a syringe and inflating the crawlers up with air and floating them about three feet off the bottom. Most of the Rainbows are still small, pound—pound and a half, but there are some that go three to four pounds. The Brookies are fairly good size, anywhere from a pound to two pounds. Every once in awhile you can get a Brown the same size. I'm not sure that DNR planted Browns because they are far and few between, but I have caught them in there.

If you have a boat or a tube and like to cast or troll, Cowbells and Little Cleos I found are the best. Silver Cowbells or blue and silver, or orange and silver Little Cleos work well. I have also used small blue or orange Rapalas trolling and did well. When trolling, I found that the deeper water is on the far side of the lake from where the trail comes in. This is an astounding  small trout lake. If you come up there after opener it's the best, and there are times you have the whole lake to yourself. I think that because it is closed all winter that come spring the fish are ready for most anything. Do you like mushrooms? There are a lot of Morell mushrooms there too, mixed among the maples and oaks. There are lots of raccoons too, so if camping, make sure you secure your coolers . . . fyi.

Now, here is a nice little trout lake to go to. It's called Pine Mountain.

It's in northern MN, just outside of a beautiful little town called Grand Marais, which is up the north shore of Lake Superior. You will need a four wheel drive to reach it, the trail is rough. Large rocks, a creek that you have to cross, and a lot of brush you have to drive through. It got its name because of the mountain you have to drive up and all the pines that surround the lake. There is a very nice place to camp, even if it is only big enough for one or two campers at a time. There's a foot path that leads to another nice campsite and that too is very small. It's best to bring a canoe, the shore line is rather brushy and the lake by the main campground is shallow.

The water there is so clean you can see down into it and the fishing is great. The Rainbows are decent size and like orange and silver Little Cleoes trolled or casted on the opposed side of the lake from the campsite. Brookies, there are many of them. Most are small, but there are some very nice ones also. And again, trolling or casting on the far side of the lake is best. They like blue and silver or maroon Little Cleoes. Still fishing from shore with night crawlers is good and a great way to have your kids enjoy the day.

There is a lot of wildlife up there. Bears might just wander into camp so you have to really take care of all your food stuff. While canoeing up there on more than one occasion, I was lucky enough to see moose swimming across the lake or on the far end of the lake feeding on the swamp grass that grows there, and loads of red squirrels everywhere.

If you do go there and are fishing in a boat, be careful and watch the weather. That area gets a lot of storms and because of the way the lake is set and its depth, when it gets bad, it gets real bad. There have been several accidents where people have drowned, but don't let that scare you off, the area is breathtaking.

That whole area is full of small trout lakes and a few larger ones that hold Lake Trout. Again, that book *Guide To Stream Trout Lakes in Minnesota* has been like a fishing bible to me, and the Gunflint Trail was like the highway to heaven.

If you follow the Gunflint Trail to the very end, there is a lodge sitting on a lake called Saganaga. That lake is very large, but to me it has the very best Walleye and Lake Trout fishing in the state. There have been record setting fish taken out of there.

If you want a small lake to fish that has large amounts of Walleyes in it while you are up in that area, try Ball Club Lake. Three of us went up there camping one time for three days. We brought with us fifteen dozen night crawlers and ten dozen Fat Head Chubs. By the end of our three days up there we had completely run out of bait. We only kept enough for our meals and tossed all the rest back. There is a small island on the lake and that's where we caught most of our fish, just drifting around that island. Nothing close to a record, but still a lot of very nice Walleyes, well worth trying. If you go farther north to the next town, Hovland, there are also some excellent fishing spots. Ester and Chester, which are trout lakes. Devilfish, which now has

Walleyes in it and breath taking palisades and excellent camping areas. If the fishing is slow and you like a lot more action, there is this river up there called the Stump River. I'm not sure if it was just a fluke or the right time of year or what, but honestly, a couple friends and I were up there and just for grins we tried that river. In a half a day of just casting yellow spoons we had caught and released over eighty small Northern Pike, anywhere from a pound to three pounds. It was fast and furious. We had bent all the barbs on the hooks so as not to harm them.

The shoreline of Lake Superior is full of streams that flow into the lake. In the fall of the year, most of those streams have Lake Trout hanging around them, along with Chinook and Coho Salmon. You could spend a lifetime trying to fish all of them. Minnesota might be called the land of ten thousand lakes, but for me, the northern lakes hold the best fishing. I truly am a northern boy.

Chapter 14

Speaking of Lake Superior, it has to be one of the best fisheries in the country. The biggest fish I have ever caught have all came from this lake and I did not need a boat or a charter service to fish it. Sure, if you have the money, a charter service can take you out and put you on the fish. They do, for the most part, a very good job. Considering they have depth finders, fish locators, and color indicators that tell you the best color to be using. They have all the equipment that you could possibly need or use. But to me, it would be like deer hunting over a bait pile. I prefer the old ways where you have to do the old trial and error method. Having more days without fish than with. That way, when you do figure it out, there is a sense of accomplishment. It gets you closer to nature and farther away from your wallet.

Please don't get me wrong, I have nothing against money or the people that have it. I have had good paying jobs and the toys that you can buy. The boats, fishfinders that I used ice fishing, snow machines, ect. It's just that it seems to me that most of the so-called hunters today are not in tune with nature and I thought that's what it's all about. Taking the time out of your busy lives to get to know nature for what it is, a beautiful thing. To go one on one with it, win or lose. I would rather go without than depend on modern technology to get it for me. To track or watch a watering hole to find what they feed on or where they bed up. It takes work, but then you earned it.

Chapter 15

Sometimes you find things totally by accident. Like one spring, my daughter came home after school and was having a bad day. I asked her if she wanted to go down to the pier and just talk. That way her brother would not be bugging her and she could tell me what was really on her mind. She said ok. Since we were going to the pier, I grabbed my fishing pole and some night crawlers. I really didn't expect to catch anything with them, but it was something to do while we were there. When we got there no one else was around, so I baited a small hook and put a small bobber on it thinking there might be some kind of pan fish there.

We were just standing there talking and wouldn't you know, something did pull my bobber under. I tried to set the hook too soon and missed the fish. I put another night crawler on and tossed it back out in the water. I had no idea what had bit on my hook, but if it happened again I was going to let it take it for a minute to make sure it had it all the way in its mouth.

We were discussing what her problem was and sure enough, it happened again. This time I was waiting for it to happen. After I thought that I had given it enough time, I reeled in the slack line and set the hook. All of a sudden this fish came shooting out of the water and the fight was on. It ran up the pier and down the pier. This fish was exciting! It fought like crazy trying to shake the hook. After what seemed like forever, it got tired enough so I could hand the pole to my daughter and so I could climb down the ladder on the outside of the pier. From there I could land the fish with my hands, because I didn't bring a net with us. It was eight feet from the top of the pier to the waterline and I didn't want it shaking off trying to just pull it up and over the wall. When I was back up on the pier, we were checking out this fish that we just caught and found out it was a Coho Salmon, just about two pounds. I never knew that they were even down there. In the next couple of hours we had a chance to talk some more and we missed a few fish and caught a couple more to take home. I think between our conversation and the fun of catching those fish my daughter was feeling better about her day.

The problems that my daughter was having were important and I was glad that we had a chance to clear things up a little, but catching those fish was a total surprise and I just could not get them out of my head. Maybe it was just a bit of good luck that there were a few fish there at that time or maybe not.

The last time that I had fished there I was using large sucker minnows for Northern Pike and that had been a bust. There was a time when the pier was full of fisherman and everyone was catching Northern Pike, but those days ended a few years back. Now the pier was empty of fishermen. When the fish quit coming in the fishermen left. I believe that when the Corps of Engineers rebuilt the pier, it messed up something that drove the Pike out of there. After all, the shipping was more important than the fishing.

Anyway, I now put my spare time into fishing there again. Not because my family really needed the fish, we didn't, but it was something to do that I enjoyed. By this time in my life, my wife had little or no interest in the things I liked to do and the kids had grown up enough that they too had better things to do than go fishing with dad. I started using different baits, casting lures, and colors. Different times of day and different weather conditions. It didn't take too long to find out that night crawlers, light line, maybe 4-pound or 6-pound test line, and small bobbers with egg hooks was the way to go. We were able to use two lines in Lake Superior, so that makes trying different things that much easier. Another way I found out was to fish Coho the same way that I fished Rainbow Trout. By floating my bait off the bottom.

Taking a small syringe and injecting air into the nightcrawler and using a slip sinker and a small split shot sinker. First, putting the slip sinker on my line, then the split shot about three feet above my hook. Injecting the crawler and casting it out, then reeling in the slack line and opening the bail, so when the fish takes the bait there is no resistance and they will just about hook themselves. This way also works for Walleyes and pretty much most fish.

In the next couple of years I was fishing down there by myself. The daily limit at that time was ten and it was easy to get. I used to get my limit and take them home, clean them, and have fish frys with my friends. I could go down to the pier and never see anyone else fishing and always have room to fish with two poles.

Until one day. I was down there fishing and had thought I would try floating a smelt off the bottom just to see what would happen. That day was clear. The water was a little dirty from a small storm that had blown through the day before. I had found that by taking my syringe and injecting air between the skin and the meat, that a smelt would float off the bottom the same way as a nightcrawler would. I had casted my smelt out there and just set my pole up against the pier, while fishing with my other pole for Cohos with a bobber. Because of the current there, you had to keep casting it out when it would float up against the pier. The other line because of the larger slip sinker would just stay where you put it.

I had spent four or more hours down there fishing, never moving my second line with the smelt on it. I was having enough fun just catching Cohos with my other line. It was getting late and I decided it was time to get home and I had four or five Cohos on the pier as it was. So, taking in my line I got my stuff together and ready to go. Then I grabbed my other line that had not moved all day, not so much as a twitch. I reeled in the slack and went to pull it up off the bottom and it seemed like it was hung up on something. I pulled up hard to clear itself and it just stayed there, not moving or doing anything. I held my rod back, trying to free it, and I felt a thump on my line. Well, snags don't thump or pull back! Man, was I excited! Then I remembered that I only had six pound test on my line and whatever was on the other end of my line had some definite weight to it. I was glad that I had just respooled my rod with brand new six pound Trilene, but never the less, I have been spooled before. (spooled-where a fish runs all the line off your reel) I reset my drag on my reel and started pulling whatever it was in to me. It was coming in like an old log. No fight, no nothing, just a head shake once in awhile. When it got close to the wall it would run out again and the drag on my reel would just sing as it was taking out line. This went on for some time, back and forth, back and forth. My arms were getting tired and I kept waiting for my line to snap or the hook to come out of the fish. But whatever it was, I knew it was also getting tired, because after a short while it's run back out to deeper water was getting slower and slower.

By now a man that had been walking the pier had noticed what I was doing and had stopped to watch and talk fishing. My arms felt like they were going to fall off and I decided that I at least wanted to see what kind of fish I had on the end of my line. So the next time I dragged it in to the wall I was going to force the issue and hope at least that I got a chance to see it. I finally got the fish right below me. I still couldn't see it, so I tightened my drag some more and started to drag whatever it was up to the surface. It fought a little bit more, but not much. We were both tired of this battle. Then I saw the tail end of this fish and knew right away what I had. It was a big Lake Trout, a very big Lake Trout. You know how your heart beats when you get real excited? Well, I thought I was going to stroke out or have a heart attack. Here I am, the biggest Lake Trout I ever had on in my life, and only six pound test line and no net. What the heck was I going to do? I got the fish up on the surface and just held him there, looking at it. The guy next to me asked me if I wanted him to hold my pole for me. I understood what he was talking about, there was only one choice for me. I had to let him hold my rod while I went over the wall and down the ladder to try to grab this fish in the gills. So, that's just what I did. I handed him my pole and over the wall I went. Remember, the water line is eight feet below me. Here I am, on the very last rung of this ladder, hanging on with one hand, and trying to slide my fingers into the gills of this large Lake Trout. He really didn't like what I was trying to do, but he was just as tired as I was, and I finally got my hand into his gills and lifted him out of the water. But now I'm standing there, hanging on with one hand, looking up eight feet to the top of the wall. This fish was using up the last of his strength flopping around trying to get back into the water and I could feel his gills and teeth cutting into my hand. So one rung at a time, I would balance myself, let go with my one hand and grab the next rung up, until I had reached the top of the wall. I was so excited that I hardly felt the pain in my hand that held this fish in the gills.

Reaching the top of the wall, I tossed the fish over, and just as I did this the hook that was in its mouth let go. I guess I was meant to catch this fish and the guy that had my fishing pole was just in awe. He said that was the largest fish he had ever seen. I think he was as excited as I was. The only thing I wished was I had a camera to take a picture of this, but of course I didn't. After a short while, I got the rest of my gear together and thanked the guy for all his help in landing this fish, that I'm sure without his help, never would have happened. Normally I let Lake Trout go. They're fun to catch, but really not that tasty. But I knew that after a fight like this, he just would have swam off and died anyway. It was very hard on both of us.

On the way off the pier there were several people walking and they all were asking me what kind of fish it was and how much it weighed. I had no idea how much it weighed, so I just guessed and told them it was twelve pounds. I knew that on the way home there was a bait shop and I was going to stop there and weigh it, just to know for sure. I got to the bait shop and the man there who knew me, because I was always getting bait and tackle from him, agreed to weigh it for me. While we were doing this, he asked me how the fishing was going and I told him that I had caught a few Coho and this large Laker. Now this is hard to believe, but God's honest truth, that Laker was sixteen and a half pounds and I caught in on six pound line and a single egg hook. I'm not sure why it happened, but it must have been destiny, because it did happen just like I have just told you. Next, what was I going to do with this huge Laker?

I left the bait shop and headed straight to my friend's house. I had an idea and needed his help. When I got to his house, he was in his garage working on a car, that's pretty much where you could find him on any given day. I told him of this Laker I had caught and asked him if I could put it in his chest freezer because it was too big to put in mine. Before I left we had made a few phone calls and had made plans to have a bbq the next weekend and the fish would be cooked then. It went off perfectly and everyone had a good time. The fish was not wasted, perfect ending to a unbelievable event.

Chapter 16

After I had caught that fish, I'm not quite sure why, but more and more people started showing up. Either my friend at the bait shop or someone I had met that day leaving the pier had said that there was fish being caught on the pier. Anyway, the next year there were so many people fishing Cohos down there it was unbelievable.

It was elbow to elbow people, and like before, everyone was catching fish. To stand back and watch was kind of cool. You would have twenty or thirty people fishing with bobbers, and at the end of a drift, depending on which way the tide was moving, everyone would reel in their lines and recast. You could have put music to it and it would have been like a choreographed fishing. You could always tell the people who knew nothing of what they were  doing. They were the ones who would cast over other people's lines. But after a few heated discussions they either learned how to go with the flow or they just never showed up again. Almost everyone got along with each other and were willing to help out any way they could. Anything to sharing bait with someone who ran out to netting someone else's fish for them. There would be people fishing Monday through Sunday, sun up to sun down. From the time the ice went out at the end of April to the last week in May. Then when the Coho and Jack Salmon would head out back to deeper water, the pier would go back to the few tourists that would come site seeing.

There was one thing that I had never told anyone and that was that after the Cohos and Jacks moved out to deeper water, the Walleyes and King Salmon would move in. Usually the first week of June for about three weeks.

Again, I would have the pier mostly to myself. Fishing them was totally different. You had to switch from crawlers to totally floating smelt, either on a float or off the bottom, and only on the farthest part of the pier in the deeper water. You had to switch your line to ten to fifteen pound test. There were some truly large fish that would come in there in that time period. We're talking ten to twelve pound Walleyes, ten to twenty pound Kings. With a Musky thrown in from time to time. The DNR had stocked a bunch of Silvers in there one year and very few people knew that. I just happened to be down there the day they did that and I never said a thing to anyone about it.

It was nothing to go down and catch a nice Walleye dinner. Three to four nineteen to twenty inch Walleyes, perfect eating size. You could cast spoons out in the sand bottom and drag it back and catch them all day long. Again, Little Cleos, half ounce, worked well for that. Copper colored, yellow or rainbow colored were among my favorites. Even with the heavier line, every once in a while I would still get a fish on that would take off after the set and never slow down or turn. They would head for deep water and nothing you did changed their mind. Lake Superior has some very large fish in it, even if they get off, that's ok. It's just the not seeing them that bugs you. I did a lot of catch and release fishing and only kept what I would eat.

Chapter 17

Here's another spot that is exciting to go to. Where Chester Creek runs into Lake Superior, right in the east end of Duluth, Minnesota. It's right off of London Road and tenth Ave East. Through the Rose Garden, across the bridge to the walking path and down to the creek. There are some large rocks that set out into the lake and the water gets kind of deep on one side of them and rocky and shallow on the other side. In the fall, the Lakers and Kings come in there to spawn. They go up the creek to feed and lay their eggs. If you get out there at sunrise, and by that I mean just as it is light enough to see, and start casting silver spoons out, keeping them right on the surface as you reel them in, the Kings will chase them and hit them hard. Or if you go out there right at dusk and for the first hour of night and cast shallow diving Rapalas, orange or blue. Jointed and about six inches long, you can catch some nice Kings. The fight is something you don't forget. They are so strong, they just run, and run fighting all the way.

Ok, the same spot but different weather, different fish. Lake Trout hang out in the same water, but the best time to catch them is when there is a strong north easterly wind. When there are six to ten foot waves crashing into the shore, standing on the rocks. You have to be careful, the waves would hit the rocks and splash right over your head. If you lost your footing and fell in they would never find your body. Lake Superior doesn't give up its dead. But putting all that aside, casting three quarter to one ounce lures into the waves and bouncing them off the bottom, it would be easy to catch your limit of three nice Lake Trout. Unless, of course, you were letting them go. Then you could catch Lakers all day.

The next way to catch Lakers and King Salmon in the fall was to fish them with spawn sacks. Floating spawn sacks off the bottom of the lake, off the mouth of the rivers. You could go to the bait shops and buy them, but I made my own. They seemed to work a lot better and you could make them any size you wanted.

I would take the spawn out of the Kings I would catch, wash them up, and put them in jars with a little Borax until I needed to make them up. First thing I needed was netting, that you could get in different colors. I liked red myself. Then you would cut it up into two inch square pieces, take some of the eggs from the jar that had the Borax in, fold up the edges, then tie it off with nylon or rag sewing thread. Some people at this point will take different colored yarn and tie that on the outside of the sack. Green, red, there are a lot of different colors to choose from. Clip off the excess netting and yarn, if that's what you want to use, being careful not to cut the thread. If you wanted to make floaters out of them, you could get Styrofoam and put small pieces of it in the sack before you put the eggs in and tied them up. There are small bags of Styrofoam balls that are the size of buckshot that also work very well. Then take the bags you made and put them in the freezer, you could pull out what you needed for the days fishing.

Lake Trout spawn works just as well. If you don't want to go through all the headache of buying all the netting and making spawn sacks, when you clean up your fish check to see if there are eggs that are not ready to come out yet. The eggs are in what is called scane, long strips of a jelled type membrane that are inside the females. You can cut the scane into nice chunks and put that on your hook and let it bounce down the bottom of the rivers. The eggs will stay together for a little while. A tasty treat for the fish, they eat that stuff right up.

Now for another little treat that this one spot has to offer in mid summer, when the lake is just about as warm as it gets. Early mornings and mid afternoons are the best times for catching large Northern Pike and Musky. When the rest of the lakes around the area have slowed down, Lake Superior still is willing to light up your life with excitement.

First, just to let you know, I fish with a St. Croix, nine-ten weight, graphite fly rod that I had converted by a man I had met who lives in the East end of Duluth, Minnesota who builds custom rods. He took a blank two piece rod and put on ceramic eyes with custom wraps. Next, I went out and got an extended fighting butt put that on, and finished it off with a South Bend reel. They don't even sell these anymore, but I was lucky enough to find two brand new ones in the box. The old, big green monsters. All ball bearings, open face. The reason I picked a St. Croix was because of sensitivity. I can feel the slightest tap of a Walleye and have enough back bone to haul in a fighting mad fifteen pound King Salmon. The more this rod bends, the stronger it seems to get. Not to mention that when it was finished, it was eleven feet long, and was perfect for shore casting spoons. Plus the lifetime warranty on the rod.

I have a number of top water lures that I use for fishing big Pike and Musky, plus I change line spools to fifteen pound test mono. I carry several interchangeable spools of line, from four pound mono to fifteen pound mono. You just never know what is going to be biting. When you go out you want to make sure you have the proper line. These top water plugs are eight to ten inches long and have triple sets of treble hooks on them. One is lime green with tiger stripes, jointed, then I have a Creek Chub that has a set of spinner blades on it. My favorite looks like a large, jointed perch. All of these float on the surface or just under it. They say that a Musky is a fish that takes a thousand casts to find. I'm inclined to agree with that. But when your arm seems like it's about to fall off because it's tired of cast after cast and when you least expect it, the water explodes!

Off of Chester Creek, I have no understanding why, but those big Musky and Northern Pike hang out there, but they do. There has to be a lot of bait fish hanging out there feeding on what comes out into the lake from the creek. I have caught a Tiger Musky that was forty three inches long. That might not be big to a lot of other Musky fisherman, but for me on a fly rod, it was pure excitement. I have also caught and released at least ten to fifteen Silver Musky that were all in the forty inch mark. They're absolutely no good to eat or at least that's how I feel, but the fight on a fly rod is just totally exciting. The Northern Pike down there are just as exciting as the Musky. They average eight to ten pounds.

One day I had a Northern on and into shore that had to be at least five feet long and there was no way that I could have spread my fingers wide enough to reach across the width of this fish. I was using a yellow and black Buck Tale with a three inch Willow Leaf Spinner. When he hit that lure, he just about pulled my rod right out of my hands. Want to talk about jaws! Well, that's what I thought I had on! When he was in shallow water I had seen him open his mouth, trying to shake the hooks out, and I swear he could have taken a small dog in one gulp. When I tried to beach him so I could measure him before I let it go, he finally shook the hooks, turned, and then he was gone. Leaving me shaking and wondering if what just happened really happened. But looking at my large Buck Tail told me the truth. That fish had straightened out the hooks on the set of trebles on the back. That was one I wish I could have at least had a chance to measure and weigh. I have read books when fisherman used to net Pike many years ago, and they talked about netting Pike six feet long and thirty pounds.

Just once I wish I could have caught one like that. And who knows, I have had fish spool me, run off a hundred yards of line, and snap it like thread. Maybe it was one of those big Pike or a very large Musky, or a fifty, sixty pound Laker, who knows? All I do know is, that I have seen and caught fish there that made me not want to go swimming in the lake anymore. It is the largest fresh water lake in the world and maybe, just maybe, there are fish in there that could take out a person. It could happen, you just don't know, do ya?

Chapter 18

Winters are long, very long, up north, unless you have something to keep you busy. I chose to ice fish. There are lots of lakes to do this. When driving around through the country, past any of the ten thousand lakes we have in Minnesota, the odds are that you will see a dozen or more ice houses on any of those lakes. I enjoy the sport myself very much and have fished my fair share of them. Once again, Lake Superior is still my favorite lake.

Around Duluth, yes, we do get some ice. Mostly pack ice and the fishing is fantastic when you can get out on it, but very dangerous. But I found a way around that and in a very nice way. Many years ago, a guy I worked with, asked me if I ever hunted or fished in Wisconsin, and at that time I had done neither of them. He asked me if I wanted to go fishing one weekend at a place called Chequamegon Bay.

It is part of Lake Superior, only in Wisconsin, just outside of the towns of Ashland and Washburn.

There are several small towns next to this bay, but to be perfectly honest, I have never met a nicer bunch of people anywhere. This bay, when frozen, over gets four to six inches of ice and gets locked in due to the shoreline. The wind cannot blow it out, so you are about as safe as you can get for being on ice.

The first of these two towns and the very first place I fished on Chequamegon Bay is the beautiful little town of Washburn. Yes, this town is small and a lot of people would go right through it and never stop, but they just don't know what they're missing. When I go there, I always eat my breakfast at this small café that has the best homemade food I have ever eaten. I get my bait, Silver Shiners, from a small bait shop just a short distance away. And at the end of the day I spend my nights at this small motel that is always very well kept up, has good nightly rates, and the people who run it are always willing to be of assistance.

To get to the bay is really easy. You just go down Central Avenue. It will take you right to a place to park your truck and then in a matter of five minutes you are on the ice. If you have never been there before and have no idea where to start fishing, all you have to do is look for the ice shacks on the ice. Or ask the guy at the bait shop there and he will tell you where you might want to start. Here is a possible starting point there. There is like a pier there. You get on the ice, walk out to the end of it, angle off to the right, and go out about three quarters of a block to a block and a half. I have fished this area several times and have done very well and have caught many three pound Splake. You are allowed to fish with up to three lines, so I would jig with one and use two tip-ups. For the tip-ups, I would make my own jigs by using a egg hook and small red Willow Leaf spinner blades just above the hook, put an Emerald Shiner on it, and drop it to the bottom. Some twenty feet down, pick it up about a foot to fifteen inches off the bottom, set up the tip-up, and go start jigging. I have used several different jigs, but the one that has worked well for me is a three inch red or orange jigging Rappala. It has hooks on it, one on each end, and then tip it with a shiner head for scent. I'd start just off the bottom and work my way up to just under the ice. I have also used half ounce Little Cleos; blue, silver, or maroon, these work quit well. I have gotten Splake, Coho Salmon, German Browns, and a Northern Pike once in awhile. There are a number of good fish out there.

If things are slow and you want to move, load up your stuff and head towards Ashland. About half way there you come to a parking area called the S Curves, right off of Bono Creek Road. Unload and be ready for a hike, for once you hit the ice you have about a quarter mile walk. Here again you are in twenty odd feet of water. Again, I would set up two tip-ups and jig with one, but now I switch to a three inch silver Swedish Pimple with a red flasher spinner, tipped with a half of a shiner. Now I have never caught a Coho Salmon here, but I have gotten Small Mouth Bass and Splake. Even though the ice will not blow out with heavy wind, you can get a whiteout and you will not be able to see the shoreline where you have your truck or car parked. A quarter of a mile in that kind of wind can be and is dangerous to your health. Been there, done that, and was very, very cold by the time I reached the parking lot.

Last but not least, the docks in Ashland. This is another small town, but like Washburn, the people there are friendly and willing to help when they can. It took a couple of years of fishing the bay to find this spot. It's right off the water markers by the large docks. I had heard that there were a lot of Walleyes in the bay, but finding them was a chore. I was down there fishing and had spotted the docks from the other side of the bay and thought I'd give it a try. I was going home the next day. By the time I found my way to the docks and got my portable ice fishing house set up, it was late in the afternoon. I was using only one rod and had set it up with an egg hook, a glow in the dark bead on top of it, a couple of split shot sinkers, and an Emerald Shiner. This I would send down to the bottom and slowly jig. The first couple fish I missed. But soon learned that as soon as I felt anything at all, I would set, and was soon catching large Smallmouth Bass. And these were very good size. And fight! It was like hooking a ten pound Pike.

It was just about totally dark. I was jigging and my line stopped dead and I set the hook. I could tell that whatever it was had some weight to it, so I played it carefully so as not to lose it. When I got it up to right under the ice, I could see that I had hooked a nice Walleye. Nothing really big, but never the less, a nice fish. About four pounds. I took out the hook, slid it back in the water, and started fishing again. I no sooner got my Shiner to the bottom and I set on another Walleye, just about the same size. I kind of wondered if it wasn't the same fish. But for the next forty five minutes I was catching Walleyes, one right after the other. The biggest one was about twenty nine inches and a good nine pounds. I had found a spot to catch Smallmouth and nice Walleyes. The stories about nice Walleyes were true, I just had to find them. Needless to say that I have returned to that spot several times after that and had done just as well. Strange though, if you are not there for that first hour of dark, you would not get a single bite from a Walleye. They just must have been on their feeding pattern and I was just lucky enough to have found a spot along their path.

Chapter 19

Up to now, every thing that I have written has been just my way of trying to explain to you, the reader, how I have turned to nature for piece of mind. As a child being left on my own and only having nature to show me that there was beauty in the world. Yes, I know that my parents put a roof over my head, fed me, clothed me, and did what was expected of them. But as far as showing me that they really cared, no, I can't say that. My mother for reasons of her own, left my father before I was old enough to remember and remarried a man that did nothing but treat her and her kids with contempt. To the point that as soon as we were able to leave home and fend for ourselves, we did, and at an age when we needed guidance the most. The age of fifteen or sixteen is way too young, but if we had not, who knows what would have happened? I can't speak for my siblings, but nature was my only out.

Fending for yourself at that age, yes, I made mistakes and lots of them. Some bad, some not so bad. But I had no role model. No one to help with making good choices versus bad choices. Never knew what love for someone else was because there was no love in my home growing up. All I had seen was cheating and physical abuse. They say that growing up is a learned behavior and that you carry on your life in the pattern that you grew up with. It has been a struggle my whole life not to be that kind of a person. I wanted to know what love was really about, but unfortunately for me, it did not happen for many years and a lot of heart breaks in between.

When I was seventeen, I was living on the streets and doing whatever I had to do to support myself. Odd jobs, hustling pool, whatever it took. I had met up with a bunch of other kids who were living basically the same way. We kind of counted on each other just to make it day to day. We used to hang out at a pool hall. That's where I made most of my money. At one time I was very good at pool. I bought my first car and paid my rent from hustling pool. Bought my first wife her wedding rings, ect. That is where I met her. She was a beautiful young woman with long black hair, beautiful eyes, just a lovely girl. We hung out together and I finally moved in with her and her mother. We ended up having our first child, got married, and thought things were ok. They weren't. Soon afterwards we both drifted apart. We tried to get back together many times, for many years, but that was not to happen. She had her lifestyle and I had mine and the two just didn't match. It took a total of nine years and three kids later before we split up for good. It was not a good split up. We ended up hating each other. Talk about a slap in the face! I saw happening to us what had happened to my parents and I didn't want my kids to have to see that. During that nine years, except for fishing, I had totally turned my back on the one thing I could count on . . . and that was nature. I swore that I would never do that again. It was only there that I could work out my problems and find peace of mind and enjoy the beauty that it has to offer.

The second attempt at what I thought was love was a total disaster. I had met this woman who had two kids from a previous marriage. At first it looked as though she enjoyed the same things that I did. In the first year we had a son together and my life changed again. I knew that no matter what, I would try my hardest and make this work because I wanted to be there and watch him grow up and be part of his life. So I decided to quit drinking and I did. Sure, I will have a drink on occasion to be sociable, but that might only happen once or twice a year. This was our first road block. She said that she gave it up but never did. Her bar life was much to important.(oh well)

It did not take too much longer after that I realized I was more of a roommate than a husband. A live in babysitter. We lived that way for fifteen years, the last eight years of which she had her own room and I had mine. We did absolutely nothing together, not even holidays. We had a nice four bedroom house on a fairly large piece of land . . . for living in town. She had her truck, I had my car. There was nothing there. But I had kept my promise to myself. I had started hunting again and spending more and more time in the woods and the lakes by myself. I think that was the only way that we lasted as long as we did. I tried to interest the kids into nature, but it never took hold, and that was ok. If you have to force someone into doing something, it just isn't going to work anyway. Please don't take this the wrong way. She was not the only person to blame for what happened. I also was not being a good person. I'm sure that there were lots of things that I could have done to change things, but didn't for one reason or another. Actually, she did the very best thing for both of us and the kids the day she left. The only thing that I wish she had done was to take all the kids and not separate them and leave one of them behind. Not wanting to be with me was acceptable, I understood that. But to leave our son behind, I never will understand that. He never did anything to deserve being left behind. He was not old enough at the time to be able to take care of himself and she would not have had the freedom to go out and hang out with her friends without having to find someone to watch our son. Enough said, not even the animals in the woods would do that. Nature takes care of their own. And you wonder why I choose nature? It was a costly experience that not only put its mark on me, but my son.

Chapter 20

Strange that in four thousand years we went from living in caves and hunting with rocks to putting a manned space station up. We went from caring and sharing for each other to caring for one's self and with little regard for everyone else. WE have people that will kill you just for looking at them the wrong way or you have a better car or nice clothes. WE start wars and kill thousands of innocent people because they don't have the same beliefs as we do. WE have stripped our planet of most of its natural resources, polluted the water, and poisoned the air we breathe. I think that as a whole, the human race has made many bad choices. If we would have paid a little more attention to nature, we would not be in the mess we are in. Just think of where we could be as a whole if we just got along with each other. At times I'm lonely, because there just are not enough people who think this way, but if I had to do it again, I would. I took time to see all that nature has to offer and it is beautiful. Simply put, I took time out to smell the roses.

Somewhere I read that we are what we are, and we are who we are. I am glad that I am who I am. Even though I came from what others would call a poor family, a dysfunctional family. When my parents decided to move out to the country into that little run down house, they gave me a gift that money could not buy. At a very early age I was allowed to open my eyes and see a whole different side of life. At first it was lonely and dark. I had been used to the sounds of living in the city and all the hustle and bustle, and no matter where you went, there was always someone around. Then it was like a whole new world was opened up and all the sounds I was used to were gone. At first it was quiet, then I started learning how to listen. The sounds were always there, I just did not pay attention to them. Like hearing the wind blow through the trees or through the tall hay in the field. Some people might say that you can't hear that, but you can, if you just listen. Listening to the sound of a robin in the morning or the sound of a flock of geese flying south for the winter. The drumming of a Partridge calling for their mate off in the distance. Even just listening to the rain falling on the roof of your house during a storm was soothing.

Not only did my hearing change, but so did my sense of smell and my eyesight. The smell of a fresh rain or freshly cut hay. Even the smell of a newly plowed field, getting it ready for the next crop. Walking past the garden and being able to smell the fresh vegetables or past the flowers my mother had planted on the side of the house. That always smelled so fragrant. When walking through the woods you could smell the pines or the cedars and even certain animals that might be near.

My eyesight has changed. Not so much that it has gotten any better. I still wear glasses, but in what I see now that I just took for granted before or just overlooked due to lack of interest. Like in the fall of the year when the leaves start turning colors. Noticing what trees are first to start changing. The reds of the oaks and maples, the yellows of the quaking aspen and poppel. The changes in the color of the ground cover. It's as if Mother Nature took out her paint box and just started mixing colors throughout the woods. The winter, when the first snowfall covers the ground with a beautiful layer of white to cover up all the shades of gray. Walking through the woods after a heavy snowfall and seeing the trees covered with layers of snow, where from just the weight of the snow the trees are bent, forming tunnels that you can walk through. Or a sleeting rain that covers the trees with a layers of ice and when the sun shines through them it's like crystal caverns. Being out on a sunny day and needing sunglasses because the ground is covered with snow crystals and the reflection of the sun is like a ground covered in diamonds.

It might seem that after reading this, that the only thing I did was to destroy the thing that I loved the most by hunting and fishing. But that is far from the truth as you can get. The animals and fish that I have taken were just for food for myself and the people I cared for. I never took more than what was necessary and always did it in the most humane way possible, so there was no suffering. In order for a person to have the success that I have had was to get to know nature. And in order to get to know nature you had to truly love and respect it for all its wonder and beauty. Hunting and fishing were not the only times I spent out in the woods. It is truly impossible for me to add up the hours or days or even years that I had spent in the woods or by the lakes and streams. I have watched many sunrises and sunsets. I've watched the fog lift off of the lakes in the early morning and the sunlight reflecting off the dew that laid on the plants and grass when walking a trail or crossing a field. I was always in awe when I would see the flocks of geese and ducks returning from their long trip south, where they went to hold up for the winter. To watch the salmon jump up and over waterfalls to get to their spawning grounds. And to even find a bear in its den hibernating.

Have you ever seen a baby loon ride on its mother's back or the birth of a fawn? Watched as a mother bear would look for food and saw her cubs playing around by her? Watched a female fox play with her young in the middle of a field? Or even watch a beaver drop a tree or drag small logs and branches to build its home? Have you ever seen an eagle swoop down right in front of you and take a fish from a river or from a lake? These are all things that I have had the honor of seeing personally and I haven't even scratched the surface. I was lucky enough to see the best part of both life and death, birth, and survival. Sure, you can watch TV and see all of these things right from the comfort of your home, but to actually witness these things sits in your sole, burns a spot in your memory. We are not alone on this planet, there is just so much more to life. But because we are what we are, we feel that we have the right to destroy our woodlands, to build condos, empty waste into our waters, and pollute the air we breathe. We just don't own any of these things nor do we have the right to destroy any of them. My kids were lucky enough to be born during a time when if they chose to, could still see these things. And even my grandchildren, if they chose to. But if we continue to think of ourselves as the only ones who have the right to survive, it won't be much longer and the upcoming generations will never get to see any of nature's best unless it is from some film archives and seen on TV. What they will consider a walk in the woods will be nothing more than a walk in some park in the middle of some town. The only water that they will know will be pumped out of some waste treatment facility that has to add more chemicals to it to make it safe for us to use. They will more than likely have to wear something on their face so they can filter out the air they breathe.

And that's only if we don't destroy ourselves first. As strange as this may sound, I feel safer walking alone in the middle of the night through a patch of woods without any source of light, than I do walking down a well light sidewalk in town.

In our past, we had a few men and women with extreme foresight. In the mid eighteen hundreds, they saw the importance of preserving our wildlife and the preservation of our woodlands. Even though they were hunters and fisherman, vast areas of land were set aside to form our greatest national treasures so that future generations could also enjoy the beauty of it. But at that time I think the reasoning behind saving our woodlands was only because of our wildlife. Not realizing that our forests, grasslands, and rainforests were all a living, breathing part of our existence. Now we know better, but is it too late? It's up to you. One voice will not be heard, but many voices will be.

1ˢᵗ buck bow hunting

www.ingramcontent.com/pod-product-compliance
Lightning Source LLC
Chambersburg PA
CBHW030402290526
45785CB00004B/1869